THE COMMUNITY OF BELIEVERS

The Community of Believers

Christian and Muslim Perspectives

A Record of the Twelfth Building Bridges Seminar

Hosted by Georgetown University at the
School of Foreign Service in Qatar
May 27–29, 2013

LUCINDA MOSHER and DAVID MARSHALL, Editors

GEORGETOWN UNIVERSITY PRESS
Washington, DC

Library of Congress Cataloging-in-Publication Data

Building Bridges Seminar (12th : 2013 : Georgetown University, School of Foreign Service in Qatar), author
    Christian and Muslim perspectives : a record of the Twelfth Building Bridges Seminar hosted by Georgetown University at the School of Foreign Service in Qatar 27-29 May 2013 / edited by Lucinda Mosher and David Marshall.
        pages cm
    Includes bibliographical references and index.
    Summary: This book presents the proceedings of the twelfth Building Bridges Seminar in Doha, Qatar in 2013, an annual gathering of Christian and Muslim scholars founded by the Archbishop of Canterbury. This volume is organized according to three major sub-themes: The Nature and Purpose of the Community, featuring essays by Gavin D'Costa on the Church and Abdullah Saeed on the Umma (nation or community); Unity and Disunity in the Life of the Community, featuring essays by Lucy Gardner and Feras Hamza; and Continuity and Change in the Life of the Community, feautring essays by Ahmet Alibasic and Brandon Gallaher. The final part of the book is a reflection by Lucinda Mosher on the spirit and tone of the exchanges between Christians and Muslims in Doha.
    ISBN 978-1-62616-196-2 — ISBN 978-1-62616-195-5 (alk. paper)
    1. Church—Congresses.   2. Ummah (Islam)—Congresses.   3. Islam—Relations—Christianity—Congresses.   4. Christianity and other religions—Islam—Congresses. I. Mosher, Lucinda, editor.   II. Marshall, David, 1963- editor.   III. Title.
BV599.B85   2013
261.2'7—dc23
                                                                                                2014026899

⊗ This book is printed on acid-free paper meeting the requirements of the American National Standard for Permanence in Paper for Printed Library Materials.

16 15   9 8 7 6 5 4 3 2   First printing

Printed in the United States of America

Cover design by Brad Norr Design.

Contents

Part III: Continuity and Change in the Life of the Community

Part IV: Reflection

Participants

Professor Asma Afsaruddin
Indiana University, Bloomington, Indiana

Professor Akintunde Akinade
Georgetown University School of Foreign Service in Qatar

Dr. Afifi al-Akiti
University of Oxford, UK

Dr. Ahmet Alibašić
University of Sarajevo, Bosnia & Herzegovina

Dr. Betül Avci
Yalova University, Turkey

The Rev. Dr. Sunil Caleb
Bishop's College, Kolkata, India Professor Gavin D'Costa, University of Bristol, UK

President John J. DeGioia
Georgetown University, Washington, DC

The Rev. Dr. Susan Eastman
Duke University Divinity School, Durham, North Carolina

Dr. Brandon Gallaher
University of Oxford, UK

The Rev. Lucy Gardner
St Stephen's House, University of Oxford, UK

Dr. Feras Hamza
University of Wollongong in Dubai

The Rt. Rev. Dr. Michael Ipgrave
Church of England

Mr. Adeel Khan
Doha International Centre for Interfaith Dialogue, Qatar

Professor Daniel Madigan SJ
Georgetown University, Washington, DC

The Rev. Dr. David Marshall
Duke University Divinity School, Durham, North Carolina

Mr. Muhammad Modassir Ali
Qatar University, College of Sharia & Islamic Studies

Shaykh Ibrahim Mogra
Muslim Council of Britain

Dr. Dheen Mohamed
Qatar University, College of Sharia & Islamic Studies

Dr. Esther Mombo
St Paul's University, Limuru, Kenya

Dr. Lucinda Mosher
Hartford Seminary, Hartford, Connecticut

Professor Abdullah Saeed
University of Melbourne, Australia

Ms. Mashal Saif
Duke University, Durham, North Carolina

Dr. Hansjörg Schmid
Academy of the Diocese of Rottenburg-Stuttgart, Germany

Professor Recep Şentürk
Fatih University, Istanbul, Turkey

Dr. Ayman Shabana
Georgetown University School of Foreign Service in Qatar

Dr. Reza Shah-Kazemi
Institute of Ismaili Studies, London, UK

Professor Philip Sheldrake
Westcott House, University of Cambridge, UK

Dr. Ayman Shihadeh
School of Oriental & African Studies, University of London, UK

Professor Janet Soskice
University of Cambridge, UK

Professor Homayra Ziad
Trinity College, Hartford, Hartford, Connecticut

Introduction

This book presents the proceedings of the twelfth Building Bridges Seminar—an annual gathering of Christian and Muslim scholars founded by the Archbishop of Canterbury in January 2002. In anticipation of his retirement as Archbishop of Canterbury at the end of 2012, Rowan Williams arranged for this project, which he had chaired since 2003, to be taken under the stewardship of Georgetown University in July of that year. Since its founding, it has been the seminar's practice to alternate between Christian-majority and Muslim-majority contexts. Thus it was under new leadership that the seminar returned for a third time to Doha—and for a second time to the Georgetown University School of Foreign Service in Qatar—in May 2013. Georgetown University president John DeGioia was present as host and participant. Assuming the role of convenor was Daniel Madigan, SJ, Ruesch Family Associate Professor in Georgetown's Department of Theology and a leading Christian scholar of Islam.

This twelfth seminar followed a well-established pattern. After a preseminar afternoon of sightseeing and fellowship, Day 1 was devoted to three pairs of public lectures. *The Community of Believers: Christian and Muslim Perspectives* includes edited versions of these lectures. Days 2 and 3 were spent in closed plenary discussion and eighty-minute sessions of small-group consideration of preassigned texts from the Bible and the Qur'an, plus a few from the Hadith.

The Community of Believers is organized according to the three major subthemes of Building Bridges 2013. Part 1, *The Nature and Purpose of the Community*, features essays by Gavin D'Costa (on the Church) and Abdullah Saeed (on the *Ummah*). D'Costa explores the tension between two themes encompassing all models of the Church's nature and purpose: the Church as mystical body of Christ versus the Church as proclamation. Saeed explains the roots and use of the term *ummah* and its development as a concept over time. In part 2, *Unity and Disunity in the Life of the Community*, Lucy Gardner offers perspectives on Christian desires for communion, experiences of division, and approaches to unity; Feras Hamza lays out the history of Muslim disunity even as the community was able to maintain cohesion in terms of its devotional and ritual praxis. In part 3, *Continuity and Change in the Life of the Community*, Ahmet Alibašić uses the Arab Spring as a case study in his discussion of accommodationism, conservativism, reformism, and militant extremism or fundamentalism as Muslim strategies in addressing the pressures of modernity. Brandon Gallaher explains the significance of the Second Vatican Council in his discussion of twentieth-century Christian ecclesiology as simultaneously an internal (*ad intra*) and external discussion (*ad extra*) of who or what the Christian Church is, and its possible responses to a "post-Christendom and also post-Christian" world.

Parts 1, 2, and 3 also include the texts foundational to small-group discussions related to that subtheme, along with the short commentaries that had been shared with the participants in advance. Biblical texts provided here are from the New Revised Standard Version. For Qur'anic material, the Pickthall translation is used (with "Allah" changed to "God"). Material in parentheses is original to the translations used; brackets surround material added by seminar staff to explain references that may not be clear to those unfamiliar with the texts.[1]

By way of conclusion, part 4, *Reflection*, is given over to "Conversations in Doha," an essay that seeks to summarize and provide a sense of the tone and style of the exchanges among participants throughout the seminar.

Readers of *The Community of Believers* may desire suggestions for further engagement with the themes on which it focuses. For wider consideration of Christian thought on the Church, a key modern text is the Vatican II document *Lumen Gentium*.[2] Also interesting to consult are Avery Dulles, *Models of the Church* (Roman Catholic); Lesslie Newbigin, *The Household of God* (Protestant); and Michael Ramsey, *The Gospel and the Catholic Church* (an Anglican attempt to hold together Catholic and Protestant understandings of the Church).[3] Those interested in works in English that would shed light on the Qur'ān texts chosen for study during the twelfth Building Bridges Seminar might wish to turn to Mustansir Mir, *Understanding the Islamic Scripture* and Neal Robinson, *Discovering the Qur'ān*. Both give much attention to sūra 2, from which our longest selection has been taken.[4] Mahmoud Ayoub's *The Qur'an Interpreted*, volumes 1 and 2, which offers a digest of Islamic commentary over the ages, covers many of the passages studied by Building Bridges 2013.[5]

Deep appreciation is extended to Georgetown University president John J. DeGioia for his ongoing support of the Building Bridges Seminar. As has always been the case, thanks are due to many people who played a role in the success of the 2013 iteration of the initiative. Samuel Wagner, coordinator for Catholic and Jesuit initiatives in the Office of the President, provided logistical support. David Marshall and Daniel Madigan were instrumental in setting the theme, organizing the circle of scholars, and choosing the texts to be studied. Reza Shah-Kazemi assisted in the selection and translation of Hadith texts. Dean Gerd Nonneman and Maya Primorac and her staff at the Georgetown School of Foreign Service in Qatar were wonderful hosts for the seminar. Georgetown University's Berkley Center—particularly director Thomas Banchoff—provide a base of operations and online presence for the seminar and have made the publication of this book possible. Finally, gratitude is extended to Richard Brown and the staff of Georgetown University Press.

Notes

1. For example, in Q. 2:120, the gloss "Muhammad" has been inserted and is in brackets: "And the Jews will not be pleased with thee [muhammad]. . . ."

2. The full text of *Lumen Gentium* is available at the Vatican website, www.vatican.va /archive/hist_councils/ii_vatican_council/documents/vat-ii_const_19641121_lumen-gentium _en.html.

3. Avery Dulles, *Models of the Church* (New York: Image Books, 1978); Lesslie Newbigin, *The Household of God: Lectures on the Nature of the Church* (London: SCM Press, 1953); and Michael Ramsey, *The Gospel and the Catholic Church* (London: Longmans, Green and Company, 1936).

4. Mustansir Mir, *Understanding the Islamic Scripture* (New York: Pearson, 2007); and Neal Robinson, *Discovering the Qur'ān: A Contemporary Approach to a Veiled Text*, 2nd ed. (Washington, DC: Georgetown University Press, 2004).

5. Mahmoud M. Ayoub, *The Qur'an Interpreted*, Vol. I (Albany: State University of New York Press, 1984); and Vol. II (Albany: State University of New York Press, 1992).

PART I

The Nature and Purpose of the Community

The Nature and Purpose of the Christian Community (the Church)

GAVIN D'COSTA

To answer the question of the nature and purpose of the Church would require an extensive historical and chronological examination to look at how different groups of Christians have answered it. The significant differences between these answers are addressed at this seminar by my colleague Lucy Gardner.[1] The differences are often seen as operating between denominational groups (Anglicans, Orthodox, Baptists, Roman Catholics, Free Church), but there are actually many internal differences within each single denomination.[2] This makes it difficult to give a single answer: "For group X, such and such is the nature and purpose of the Church." Difficult, but not impossible. One other difficulty presents itself: why not go back to the Bible and give a biblical answer? Surely all Christians are united on the authority of the Bible? However, Paul Minear, in *Images of the Church in the New Testament*, shows how ninety-six biblical images bring into focus differing aspects of the Church, and I am not convinced that Christians are united on the "authority" of the Bible.[3] While the plurality we find in different Christian denominations is a partial reflection on biblical pluralism, all Christians are called to be "one." From a certain point of view, which I share, divided Christian churches are a "scandal."[4]

I should also declare my own starting point: I am a Roman Catholic Christian who is married to a Quaker. That presents me with lots of challenges but a wonderful opportunity to learn about radically different ways of trying to be "church."

I'd venture that two guiding themes encompass all the models of the nature and purpose of the Church, even when there is severe tension between some of them: (1) The nature and purpose of the Church is for Christians to grow more Christlike through following and submitting to the call of God, through the power of the Holy Spirit, and through mutual support, prayer, and praise—i.e., the Church as a school of friendship: with God and with neighbors; (2) the nature and purpose of the Church is for Christians to share this Trinitarian gift through word and deed, and to share this in a Christlike manner. Each sub-model gives a particular flavor to the two themes and draws them out differently. The actual history of the Church can be criticized by both themes at different times. This is inevitable and reflects the Church as a human community. But it is not just a human community.

In an attempt to be as ecumenical and "mainstream" as possible, given the limits of time, I've decided to oversimplify and focus on two major "models" of the Church that have lasting currency—and submodels within the main: (1) the Church as mystical body of Christ and (2) the Church as proclamation.[5]

The Church as Mystical Body of Christ

The Orthodox and Roman Catholic Churches are often associated with this model, although by no means exclusively. The model stems from a number of New Testament passages that identify the community of Christians with the "body of Christ." For example, in Ephesians 4:16, St. Paul says: "speaking the truth in love, we will grow to become in every respect the mature body of him who is the head, that is, Christ. From him the whole body, joined and held together by every supporting ligament, grows and builds itself up in love, as each part does its work." This became a key organic metaphor upon which the notion of "body of Christ" was developed, including sometimes associating the "head" with the "episcopacy" (bishops), or even a particular part of the episcopacy (the Pope).[6]

The power of metaphors is precisely in generating new ways of seeing things.[7] We can notice this dynamic in virtually all the key biblical images: they can be read in one way, and then another. Further, Paul, in the account given in Acts 9: 3–4, makes this interesting identification of the Christian community with Christ himself at the point of his conversion. He had been persecuting Christians, you will recall. He was good at it. Then, on the road to Damascus, "suddenly a light from heaven flashed around him. He fell to the ground and heard a voice say to him, 'Saul, Saul, why do you persecute me?' 'Who are you, Lord?' Saul asked. 'I am Jesus, whom you are persecuting,' he replied." The "voice" does not identify the historical Jesus with his body while on earth, but with his body the Church takes on a function of Jesus after his resurrection. I hope you can see the seed of the idea present. The seed would lead in many directions.

Before proceeding, it might help to make a tentative distinction between the horizontal dimension (sociological and historical snapshots of Christian communities) and the vertical dimension (God's dealings with his community). When asked, "How could any group that acts like that (*that* being apartheid, slavery, etc.) claim they are the body of Christ?", the question, if not anachronistic, operates on using the horizontal to judge the vertical dimension. If asked too often, the vertical dimension is rightly called into question. But logically the vertical's veracity is not dependent on the horizontal's alignment. The vertical and horizontal always intersect so things are more complex, but these models work primarily on the vertical dimension.

If the Church "is" the "body of Christ," does it mean that in some sense Christians are claiming divinization—as they believe Christ was both human and divine? One has to answer this carefully, even if there were not so many Muslims in the room. The Greek Orthodox Church does speak about *theosis*, divinization, but it does not mean that the created order loses its created status. It means that the created order participates with, lives out of, and is transformed by the divine energies (not the divine essence). Participating in the divine life, the invisible energies of God, turns the created order like wood and pigments that make paint into an *icon*, a holy image, a sign that can point us to a reality. But it also turns the created order, persons, into saints whose lives fully reflect God's life. The body of Christ here is a deeply material model, which indicates that by looking at these bodies, the performed lives of the saints, their relics, and the places they lived and acted, we glimpse the Christlike power that we also can share and inhabit. The daring word *theosis* is used to bring out the nature and purpose of the mystical body: that in our becoming part of that body we begin, or try, to make an ascent toward the saving and redeeming God. The ascent is finally dependent on grace but also requires human actions.

This is why a cognate image also became so important to Christians: the Church as the spouse of Christ. If we have body images, we have the possibility of erotic images! The scriptural text of *The Song of Songs* explores the complex moves of the lover's burning heart and bodily senses in a quite remarkable fashion. Some of the commentaries domesticate the text, but traditionally the Church is seen as the lover being united to Christ. He is the male; the Church becomes female. He gives his body in the Eucharist; those who receive him continue in this state of marriage. This nuptial imagery was central to the early Church and was revived by recent popes but had always been strong in the Orthodox traditions.[8]

But the body image also evokes the material source of all bodies: the maternal. This maternal thematic also arose from the scriptural account in John's

Gospel, where Jesus on the Cross "gives" his mother into the care of the beloved disciple and the beloved disciple into the care of Mary (John 19:26–27).[9] From very early on Mary was understood as the archetype of the Church: the maternal body that nourishes and feeds her children, who guides them by example: the contemplation of the divine within and without.[10]

I've given attention to these images because they bring out vividly the personal and affective elements of "church belonging" that relate to such primal human instincts: love, affection, nurture, and growth as well as discipline, punishment, trial, and struggle. And beyond these: peace and rest. But the personal always requires structures, rituals, discipline, and formation.[11]

Another trajectory out of the mystical body of Christ led to the view of the Church as the "Sacrament of Christ" or "the sacrament of salvation." The invisible God must communicate to people through visible signs. Visible signs start with creation, and the story of the history of revelation runs from creation to Israel, and then finally to Christ.[12] If a sign points to other than itself, Christ is a symbol or icon—where the sign is also the signified. This is a Latin way of putting it. The Greeks prefer icon, drawing on Paul's assertion that "Christ is the icon of the invisible God, the firstborn over all creation." (Col. 1:15) They both get at the same thing: the Church is the visible sign of Christ to the world. You clearly need glasses in careful focus for this to work!

The early Christians believed that Christ had left them rituals and signs that shaped them into being more Christlike: what would later be called sacraments. Both the East and West eventually held that Christ instituted seven sacraments, rituals that confer special grace, "essential," even "necessary," aids for the spiritual journey. These sacraments related to the earthly pilgrimage: birth—baptism; adulthood—confirmation; Eucharistic meetings; confession; marriage; religious consecrated life and priestly ministry—holy orders; illness and death—last rites. The two repeatable ones become central: confession, for the forgiveness of sins; and the Eucharist, as Christ's gift of himself for our salvation.[13] For each and every sacrament there has been considerable dispute as to its form (the words and materials used), when it is to be conferred (baptism for infants or only adults), its meaning (a sign, a symbol, an ontological transformation of matter, etc.), and whether Jesus really instituted it. The Reformation intensified some existing earlier disputes but also raised new ones.[14]

Rituals can easily become rote and mechanical. Rituals can lead to near obsession to performing the liturgy "correctly." In reaction we find some Christian communities dispensing with liturgical form almost altogether. This can be seen dramatically in unstructured Quaker "worship." No sacred text is read, no rituals are conducted. Rituals can also minimize the interior drama and complexity of how God's grace works as the focus becomes fixed on external rites. In reaction we find some communities that emphasize personal transformation. Here religious worship might consist of numerous testimonies of how people's lives have been changed by God and be punctuated by spontaneous prayers and singing and even ecstatic dance and joy. Finally, sacred rituals can allow those who control the dispensing of sacraments, priests, to abuse their powers. In response we see reforming groups that dispense with "sacred ministers" and instead have a common ministry of all baptized.

A related image that takes us into dangerous territory is the Church as the "ark of salvation"—the place where saving grace is found in a world beset by sin. The Greeks did not hold to "original sin," and the Latin view of original sin did not mean "total depravation," as it would for many Calvinists. Nevertheless, for all three groups, entering the Church was like walking on to the ark—and just in time. There was a positive and important dimension to this model: Christ had come to save the world, and the location of this saving action was to be found in the Church—not necessarily because of its own virtue but because of its transmitting (and for some, enacting) the words and deeds of Christ. In the Latin West, this also became formulated in the teaching *extra ecclesiam nulla salus* (there is no salvation outside the Church).[15] It is important to raise this point in the midst of a Muslim audience because, historically, the implications of this teaching were eventually seen to relate to Muslims (who, it was often thought, had freely and knowingly rejected the truth of the gospel by virtue of being Muslim).[16]

This latter assumption—that everyone who is not a Christian has willfully rejected Christianity—is difficult to defend today. We find a new twist to *extra ecclesiam nulla salus* tradition at the Second Vatican Council (1963–65). This was convened by the Roman Catholic Church, and its doctrinal teachings have authority over Catholics. In *Lumen Gentium* (The Dogmatic Constitution on the Church), paragraph 14, the no salvation teaching is reiterated but sharply contextualized: "Whosoever, therefore, knowing that the Catholic Church was made necessary by Christ, would refuse to enter or to remain in it, could not be saved." In one very real sense, the teaching applies most profoundly to Roman Catholics—and perhaps especially to Catholic theologians—for they are now clearly aware of this necessity. (Many Catholics do not read these documents!) The same document also says unambiguously that those outside the Church through invincible ignorance of the gospel may be saved (*Lumen Gentium*, par. 16). It does not say how, and it does not explicitly attribute this possibility to the religions of those people who may be saved. Neither does it deny their religions a role in this process. One other interesting thing about *Lumen Gentium*, paragraph 16, is that—like the World Council of Churches some years previously—it rejects the teaching that the Jews as a nation are cursed because they killed Jesus. It also acknowledges the church's special relationship with the Jewish people as it is dependent on their race (Jesus and Mary were both Jewish) and their scripture (the "Old" Testament). But, and I can't go into this now, it also then mentions Muslims, with whom the Church has a special relationship through a shared worship of one God and the mutual esteem of Abraham. Paul VI had used the term "religions of Abraham" that John Paul also employed. We see in this document the largest Christian Church in the world struggling with its own traditions in the light of religious pluralism.

The missionary history of the "ark of salvation" has plenty of uncomfortable and inglorious moments. That must be stated unambiguously. However, it is also central to the nature and purpose of the Church that it exists not for itself but for the whole world. In the Latin West, this view of the Church was a great engine driver for mission, but the Latin West was also closely tied to imperial conquests. Joseph Conrad's famous image of "the torch and the sword" haunts the modern western imaginary where the spread of Christianity is seen as entwined with the destruction of civilizations, the rape of cultures, and the imposition of its own image (western Latin Christian) onto the world. I myself may be perceived as one of those alleged "victims" of that imperial missionary conquest! But personally, I do not think I am a victim. I'm very grateful to those Portuguese missionaries who traveled to India and wanted to share the greatest good they had discovered. The reality of mission is far more complicated. It is well worth defending and needs defense within some groups of contemporary Christians.[17]

Underlying these deeply spiritual images there is unmistakably the question of the church as institution. This has arisen often in "battles" about Christian identity. Some of these discussions were supported by military and political power and make for painful memories. Robert Bellarmine, a great Counter-Reformer, famously defined this visibility as being as "palpable as the community of the Roman people, or the Kingdom of France, or the Republic of Venice." When Bellarmine said "Church," he meant the "perfect society" in a twofold sense: it was subordinate to no other society, and it had the fullness of salvation already given to it. When he said visible church, like the "Republic of Venice," he was keen to be able to say who was a Venetian and who not. For him the Church of Rome, under the papacy, was the only true visible true church. "Church" as institution has come to be viewed as the legal, juridical, clerical, and institutionalized elements of the "nature" of the church.

In our modern age, where there is general skepticism about many, if not all, institutions, this aspect has been criticized by many theologians. But this aspect returns through the back door in any discussion about ecumenism. As with marriage, there are laws and rules that develop when people want to safeguard some cherished social practice precisely because of its value. The greatest strengths of the "institutional" are bringing "order" into community life, providing strong communal identity, and highlighting enduring elements in a time of transition and change. Its greatest weaknesses are the freezing of a particular order into a permanent state of affairs and suppressing questions and experiments related to that order as well as failing to see that legal and juridical life are only one part of the picture.

In the models and images I have described, differences exist between the Roman Catholic / Orthodox communions and some of the low churches of the Reformation. The Reformation was a complex movement that included "high" Churches that kept sacraments (varying numbers) and priests or ministers (varying degrees, but were first to include women). The Anglican Church, so important to Building Bridges, is technically not a Reform Church. It has different roots for its protests against Rome. Hence, the images I have mentioned are found widely among different Christians.

I have spoken about the Church as mystical body, as spouse, as sacrament, as ark of salvation, and as institution. I lumped all these under the "body of Christ." I need to attend to two further images that have great significance and relate to the preaching of Christ and his good works toward the poor. I turn to my second main model.

The Church as Proclamation

You will have noticed the logic of these models: in pointing to Christ, there is an inevitable pointing to one's own community, a certain risky celebration of human institutions and practices—as it would appear to some. The major split in Western Christendom happened with the Reformation, and, as the name indicates, it was about reforming (and questioning) the Church and rethinking forms of discipleship. It would be crass to attribute the following two models to the Reformers; but perhaps their strong emphasis on these models was their special charism. These themes are to be found in the ancient churches as well, but the Reform brings a real energy and action to these themes.

Karl Barth is one of the best formulators of the view that restlessly and relentlessly argues that the sole purpose and nature of the Church is to point to the gospel, to Christ, and not to itself. He saw in the Roman Catholic Church an unhealthy focus on itself, epitomized in the centrality of the "analogy of being." This used the created world as the base for God-talk according to Barth, rather than Christ as the basis. He saw this analogy as the invention of the "anti-Christ."[18] Barth's was Christological through and through: the only clue for speaking about God was Christ, and Christ was judgment over the world, especially and including the Church. Christ also stood as a judgment over all religions as "idolatry," for they are human-made, unless and until they preach Christ crucified and risen. Here again the nature of the community entails a judgment on all communities.

Further, Barth's Lutheran emphasis on preaching the cross turned into a razor-sharp critique against the Church's pretensions toward worldly power and status, and a constant call to the Church to do what it was created to do: repent and reform, and preach Christ. While Barth is sometimes presented in this very Christological light, it should be remembered that his massive final opus was titled *The Church Dogmatics*. His iconoclasm did not mean that he was against the Church as community. On the contrary. But he understood the formation of the community toward this single goal: repentance and reform so as to worship and preach the true triune God. Barth firmly believed that the Church itself required evangelizing so that it could properly be a missionary church. The inward turning was also and always an outward turning. The proclamation was centered on the Word of God, the preaching of the scripture.

One of the hugely attractive elements of this type of model of the Church is that it joins in with the critique of the Church. It does not end up in a defensive posture as has happened too often with the Latin Church of the West (and sometimes of the Eastern Churches). When you have names like "mystical body of Christ," it can be difficult for those within to criticize their communion. But when you drop this name and employ a different model, reform and change are much easier; or at least easier in the early days of reform and change! The whole issue of continuity is discussed in an essay in this volume by my colleague Brandon Gallaher, so I will leave this for now.[19]

At the very same time of Barth's writing, there also arose out of a similar Lutheran theology of the cross an emphasis on God, who became abject and forsaken in Christ. This abject and forsaken humanity, experienced by the human nature of Christ, brought out a special solidarity with the abject and forsaken of the earth. Many Christians felt it was time to retrieve the model, drawing upon Isaiah's "Servant Songs," of the Church as Suffering Servant. The two world wars in Europe knocked the confidence out of many Western Christians: the Churches had butchered the Jewish people; the "colonies" were demanding freedom and were providing a powerful critique against European and Christian expansionism; and the heart of Christian Europe had succeeded in destroying itself. Among many of the Reform theologians a new emphasis was placed on "social action" arising out of the gospel, rather than preaching but acting as the church had done. Words seemed hollow in the light of recent Christian actions. In Catholic circles, this thematic was typically later in arriving, but it came in a different form: liberation theology that emphasized the Church's mission as being toward social and political liberation and joining forces with whatever liberative powers that existed in society. In Latin America these allies were often Marxist oriented, and in Sri Lanka, Buddhist believers. In South Africa, Muslims and Christians had already joined hands well before in resistance to apartheid. The social gospel and the kingdom of God, understood as justice and peace, were what the Church was all about. A very famous Catholic theologian, Leonardo Boff, came into conflict with his own Church precisely when he turned this liberation theology critique of hierarch and power to analyze the Catholic Church as a society. Another interesting aspect of this view of Church is that it took a powerful grip of many Roman Catholic missionary movements that focused on what was called "humanization." It was left to various Protestant groups to pursue "mission" as it had been traditionally understood.

As with all the models, there are strengths and weaknesses. The obvious strength is that Jesus's own ministry was marked with action and deeds, witnessing to a new liberative and redeeming power and creating communities in which repentance and love were to be central. Words alone without action are hollow. Another strength is that this model responds to one of the fiercest critics of Christianity: Marxism, which was also in the business of caring for the poor.

Two weaknesses might be mentioned. Critics argue against this model that the gospel had been turned into a political ideology or into a social agenda that misses that the kingdom of God was solely about God's actions, not human action. Other critics argue that while the gospels do preach unbounded charity, this follows from faith and is not faith itself. The Christological act of faith had lost its central role in this type of model.[20]

Conclusion

I want to make one banal closing comment and one partisan closing comment, but only in the spirit of stimulating discussion. The banal observation is that all these models have strengths and weaknesses. They may help Christians appreciate each other and what they have in common while trying to be "Church." It may also help others understand the complex task of the nature and purpose of the Christian community. The partisan comment is that, as a Roman Catholic, I am forced to struggle with the claim made in *Lumen Gentium* (para. 8 and 14), that the Church of Christ "subsists" most fully in the Roman Catholic Church. This is an uncomfortable claim to make within such a distinguished ecumenical audience, and an uncomfortable claim to make by someone who knows the Catholic Church from birth! Nevertheless, if it were true, what might it mean about the ways and the mechanisms by which the models discussed here might balance and mutually correct themselves within a single institution? This is a question about ecumenism in one way, and about how ecumenism is construed within one community that aspires to be a universal church to represent One Lord on earth.

Notes

1. See Lucy Gardner, "Perspectives on Christian Desires for Communion and Experiences of Division," in the present volume.

2. According to the Center for the Study of Global Christianity at Gordon Conwell Theological Seminary, there are approximately forty-one thousand different Christian denominations (study based on statistics from 2011; see http://christianity.about.com/od /denominations/p/christiantoday.htm, accessed April 2013).

3. See Paul Minear, *Images of the Church in the New Testament* (Louisville, KY: Westminster John Knox Press, 2004); and also Joseph Ratzinger, "Biblical Interpretation in Crisis: On the Question of the Foundations and Approaches of Exegesis Today," ed. Richard J.

Neuhaus, *Biblical Interpretation in Crisis* (Grand Rapids, MI: Eerdmans, 1989), 1–23, and the other essays. Compare Ratzinger's notion of the authority of the Bible with the historical critical approach of John Barton. See John Barton and Robert Morgan, eds., *Biblical Interpretation* (Oxford: Oxford University Press, 1988).

4. In the Second Vatican Council, the Roman Catholic Church views the lack of full Christian institutional unity as a "scandal." See "Decree on Ecumenism," paragraph 1, in Norman Tanner, *Decrees of the Ecumenical Councils*, Vol. 2, *Trent to Vatican II* (London: Sheed & Ward, 1990), 908. However, it envisages some form of Petrine unity as the minimal visible sign of unity.

5. I'm particularly indebted to Avery Dulles SJ, *Models of the Church. A Critical Assessment of the Church in All Its Aspects* (Dublin: Gill & MacMillan, 1976), for the notion of models and how they might work. I am not in agreement with some of his judgments, but neither was Dulles himself in later life. On this, see Darius Jankiewicz, *The Magisterium and Theologians in the Writings of Avery R. Dulles: The Conflicting Legacy of the Second Vatican Council* (Saarbrücken: Verlag Dr Müller, 2009).

6. See Thomas Aquinas on this, which is well summarized and systematically explicated by George Sabra, *Thomas Aquinas' Vision of the Church. Fundamentals of an Ecumenical Ecclesiology* (Mainz: Matthias-Grünewald-Verlag, 1987); and also with more attention to the institutional dimension in Colman O'Neill, "St. Aquinas on the Membership of the Church," *Thomist* 27 (1963): 88–140.

7. See Janet Martin Soskice, *Metaphor and Religious Language* (Oxford: Clarendon Press. 1987), which contains a rich treatment of this subject.

8. Aspects of John Paul II's nuptial imagery have been severely criticized by some Catholics and heralded by others. The Orthodox employment of this and its Marian tradition can be found, for example, in Sergius Bulgakov, *The Burning Bush: On the Orthodox Veneration of the Mother of God* (Grand Rapids, MI: Eerdmans, 2009); and, more importantly, in Bulgakov, *The Bride of the Lamb* (Grand Rapids, MI: Eerdmans, 2001). A provocative and helpful discussion of the feminine images with Catholic ecclesiology can be found in Tina Beattie, *God's Mother, Eve's Advocate* (London: Continuum, 2002).

9. "When Jesus saw his mother, and the disciple whom he loved standing near, he said to his mother, 'Woman, behold, your son!' Then he said to the disciple, 'Behold, your mother!' And from that hour the disciple took her to his own home."

10. The connection between Mary and Islam is important, given the meeting at which this essay was presented initially. During discussion at the Second Vatican Council on the relationship of Islam and Catholicism, Archbishop Joseph Descuffi raised this point about Mary. What is startling is his envisaged special relationship with Islam because of Mary, more so than with Judaism: "They [Muslims] affirm his many miracles, his miraculous birth. They recognize the Immaculate Conception of the Blessed Virgin Mary, her purity and virginity, her singular perfection, and, praying to her as their Mother with a sincere and devout heart, they confidently ask of and obtained from her remarkable favors, healings and even miracles. . . . What I am now saying is not the figment of my imagination or the product of exaggeration in the hope of some gain, but the fruit of ten years' experience, what I've seen for myself in Ephesus, in the place called by *Panaga Kapula*, i.e., the House of Mary, Our Lady Mary. For the last ten years I have seen about 100,000 Muslims throughout the year join the same number of Christians and together with them . . . venerate the Virgin Mary the Mother of Jesus. . . . If we may add to these particular facts the fact that Muslims observe the natural law of the Decalogue, fasting, alms giving and prayer, we can say that we find them closer to

us than the Jews." Quoted in Andrew Unsworth, *A Historical and Textual-Critical Analysis of the Magisterial Documents of the Catholic Church on Islam: Towards a Hetero-Descriptive Account of Muslim Belief and Practice* (Ph.D. dissertation, Heythrop College, London, 2007), 146.

11. Talal Asad develops this view in *Genealogies of Religion: Discipline and Reasons of Power in Christianity and Islam* (Baltimore: Johns Hopkins University Press, 1993). More ecclesiologically, in terms of sociopolitical intervention in the same vein, see Armando Salvatore, *The Public Sphere. Liberal Modernity, Catholicism, Islam* (New York: Palgrave, 2007).

12. Recently Islam has been thought of by some theologians as being part of this revelatory/salvation history, but even then, for most who do, they still see it like Judaism: pointing toward Christ. David Marshall carefully outlines some of these positions in his *Roman Catholic Approaches to the Qur'ān since Vatican II*, http://repository.berkleycenter.georgetown.edu/120711MarshallRomanCatholicApproachesQur%E2%80%99anVaticanII.pdf.

13. On the Eucharist constituting the Church in East and West, see Paul McPartlan, *The Eucharist Makes the Church: Henri de Lubac and John Zizioulas in Dialogue* (Edinburgh: T& T Clark, 1993).

14. One particular advantage of this model is that it is able to respond to the age-old critique: there are so many sinners in the Church and the history of the Christian church is hardly a visible sign of grace. Defenders of this model might respond, as Paul did, that "he that eateth and drinketh unworthily, eateth and drinketh damnation to himself, not discerning the Lord's body" (1 Cor. 11: 29, King James Version). The holiness of the Church lies in the sacraments. The Latin West's famous definition of the sacraments as *ex opere operato* (Council of Trent) signaled their objective efficacy, like Christ, with the offer of grace not being dependent on the sinlessness of the minister or the recipient, but being dependent on Christ's promise to those who come in repentance and humility.

15. See Francis A. Sullivan, *Salvation outside the Church? Tracing the History of the Catholic Response* (London, Geoffrey Chapman, 1992).

16. I treat this matter in some detail in Gavin D'Costa, *Vatican II and Other Religions* (Oxford: Oxford University Press, 2014).

17. See Lamin Sanneh, *Translating the Message: The Missionary Impact on Culture* (Maryknoll, NY: Orbis Books, 1989); and Brian Stanley, *The Bible and the Flag* (Leicester, UK: Inter-Varsity Press, 1990). who avoid falling into clichéd criticism of mission.

18. For Barth on analogy, see Hans Urs von Balthasar, *The Theology of Karl Barth*, trans. Edward T. Oakes (1951; repr. San Francisco: Ignatius Press, 1992). One of Barth's best expositors, other than himself, is to be found in the work of John Webster.

19. See Brandon Gallaher, "The Christian Church Facing Itself and Facing the World: An Ecumenical Overview," in the present volume.

20. See Ratzinger's critique of liberation theology in *Church, Ecumenism and Politics: New Essays in Ecclesiology* (New York: Crossroads, 1988). Regarding the emergence of a theological politics in contrast to political theology, see John Howard Yoder, *The Politics of Jesus* (Grand Rapids, MI: Eerdmans, 1972).

The Nature and Purpose of the Community (*Ummah*) in the Qur'ān

I n this essay I will explore the meaning of *ummah* (community). I will use two key Qur'ānic texts to examine its nature and purpose. I will also draw from the Qur'ānic texts that make reference to the concept of *ummah*, and from some Qur'ānic commentaries that address interpretation of these Qur'ānic texts. Together these sources will give a sense of how the concept of *ummah* is understood in Muslim tradition. Given the extensive range of Qur'ānic interpretations that make reference to *ummah*, I will be very selective. From the early period of Qur'ānic exegesis, I will draw on the work of key figures like Ṭabarī and Rāzī. From the modern period, I will outline the work of three central figures—Asad, Mawdudi, and Quṭb—without aiming to cover specific issues in any depth.

Roots and Use of the Term *Ummah*

The Qur'ān uses the term *ummah* to refer to community. Although there is some uncertainty about the roots of the term, some commentators suggest that it is derived from the Arabic root *umm*, which means mother, or its verbal root, *amma*. Other scholars associate the term *ummah* with the notion of imam, or leader. For others, however, the word is not actually derived from Arabic but is probably of Hebrew or Aramaic origin.

To begin the exploration of this concept, I will first make note of the numerous Qur'ānic references to *ummah*. The Qur'ān refers to the term just over sixty times. The vast majority of these references are from the Meccan period of revelation, and a relatively small number from the Medinan period. The term is deployed in the Qur'ān to describe many different kinds of community and is not restricted to the Muslim community. *Ummah* as a term is versatile: it has been used to refer to a group of people who follow a particular religion (Qur'ān 5:48); the followers of prophets (10:47); the beliefs of a particular group of

15

people (43:22); and even just a group of people (28:23). It has also been used to refer to a group of people within a larger community (3:113); to describe a misguided group of people (43:33); and to refer to a group of people who are misguided among the followers of a prophet (27:83). Furthermore, *ummah* has also been used to refer to a period of time (11:8) and to refer to communities of nonhuman beings, such as birds and land animals (6:38). These are just some of the many usages of the term.

Development of the Concept of *Ummah*

The concept of *ummah* developed over time. It began as a broad and inclusive concept but has developed into one that is more exclusivist and specific.

The Pre-Islamic Concept of Community

The relation between the Qur'ānic concept of *ummah* and the pre-Islamic concept of the community is revealing. The pre-Islamic conception of community was ethnically based and inherently tied to a sense of tribal identity. These tribal communities or networks afforded protection and security. In this sense, tribal protection was a key structuring principle for pre-Islamic communities. When Islam emerged, the Prophet and the Qur'ān promoted a new form of communal bond. The basis of identity in the new community was faith, which transcended the tribal affiliation of the Arabs.

Ummah during the Time of the Prophet

In the Meccan and early Medinan Qur'ānic passages, the term *ummah* is deployed in varying ways, all of which are relatively general. When referring to the community of the believers, *ummah* seems inclusive insofar as anyone who believed in God was considered to be part of the *ummah*. This appears to be the usage in the Medina document (usually referred to as the "Medinan Constitution"), where Jews are referred to as an *ummah* with the believers. The central belief in God remained the foundation of the community, such that any person could be included in the *ummah* so long as they believed in one God. This meant that people from Jewish or Christian backgrounds could be considered part of the *ummah*, alongside the followers of the Prophet Muhammad. Accordingly, particular categories or religious identities are not as important as the overarching imperative of *tawḥīd* (belief in the oneness of God).

However, from the mid-Medinan period onward, the *ummah* came to be understood more narrowly as referring to the community of the Prophet Muhammad. This community increased in Medina, with its distinct rituals, practices, and sense of a political community. Its sense of community grew out of struggles on theological, political, and military fronts. This was particularly defined in its struggle with the Meccan polytheists and the Jewish community of Medina, through which the Muslim community gradually emphasized its distinct identity. Clearly, the Prophet Muhammad and Muslims needed time for a distinct idea of *ummah* to develop, with its own shared beliefs, understandings, rituals, and eventually its own institutions.

Postprophetic Understandings of *Ummah*

After the death of the Prophet, the concept of the *ummah* continued to develop, acquiring characteristics that had not existed during the prophetic period. For instance, the *ummah* became closely associated with political and state power, whereas in the prophetic period the *ummah* was primarily associated with shared faith and belief in one God. In the prophetic period, there was comparatively little emphasis on the political dimension of the *ummah*, which was to be acquired in a significant way during the period of the Rāshidūn caliphs. With the expansion of the Muslim community into North Africa and the Middle East, the notion of the *ummah* became connected with the expansionism of the Muslim state. In this way it came to denote a religious and a political community that nevertheless remained unconnected to any particular ethnicity or geographical location.

Key Characteristics of Community in the Qur'ān: Classical Commentators

In many Qur'ānic commentaries this community is seen as being based primarily on faith in God. It is described as fair and just, and a community that seeks to promote good and forbid evil. This can be seen in detail in the commentaries for two key Qur'ānic texts: 2:143 and 3:110. I first examine the stance taken by early commentators of these sections and then compare these with more modern interpretations.

The "Best *Ummah*" in Q. 3:110

The Qur'ān makes reference to the Muslim *ummah* as being the best community, having evolved for the service of humankind. This *ummah* enjoins what is right and forbids what is wrong and is centered on belief in God. This depiction of the *ummah* is explicated in a number of Qur'ānic verses, but most significantly in Qur'ān 3:110: "[Believers], you are the best community singled out for people: you order what is right, forbid what is wrong, and believe in God. If the People of the Book had also believed, it would have been better for them. For although some of them do believe, most of them are lawbreakers."[1] In relation to this verse, the Qur'ān commentator Abū Ja'far Muhammad b. Jarīr al-Ṭabarī (d. 310/923) provides several interpretations of "best *ummah*": (a) those who migrated with the Prophet from Mecca to Medina or more generally the companions of the Prophet; (b) those Muslims who have the attributes of enjoining what is good, prohibiting what is evil, and believing in God; (c) and the entire *ummah* of the Prophet Muhammad. The latter, which is also attributed to al-Ḥasan al-Baṣrī, seems to be Ṭabarī's preferred interpretation.[2]

Fakhr al-Dīn al-Rāzī (d. 606/1209), another Qur'ān commentator and theologian, asks why the Muslim *ummah* is given preference, given that other communities also commanded good, forbade evil, and believed in God. He concludes that the Muslim *ummah* command good and forbid evil in the most emphatic manner, and are willing to use force to do so. He states that while one can command good and forbid evil by one's heart, tongue, or hand, the strongest means to do so is fighting.[3] Similarly, Ibn Kathīr (d. 774/1373) emphasizes that "Allah states that the *ummah* of Muhammad is the best nation ever," and draws on ḥadīth to make his point. In particular, a ḥadīth that Bukhari recorded in which Abū Hurayrah (one of the famous first-generation Muslims) reportedly commented on this verse, saying "[You, Muslims, are] the best nation of people for the people, you bring them tied in chains on their necks [capture them in war] and they later embrace Islam."[4]

This is a rather curious way of emphasizing the *ummah* as the best community, and it does not necessarily receive support from other scholars. Ṭabarī, for example, is clearly against this position. He interprets this "preference" as relating to the issues of commanding others to do good by believing in God and His messenger and observing the laws of God; and of avoiding evils by forbidding *shirk* (associating other beings with God), not rejecting God's messenger, and avoiding the doing of those things that God has prohibited.[5]

The Purpose of the "Middle Nation": Q. 2:143

Surah 2, verse 143, identifies the key characteristics of this *ummah*: a community of *wasaṭ* (meaning "middle," "fair," and "just") that enjoins whatever is right and forbids whatever is wrong. The verse says, "We have made you [believers] into a just community [literally 'a middle nation'] so that you may bear witness [to the truth] before others and so that the Messenger may bear witness [to it] before you."

This translation by Abdel Haleem renders the Arabic phrase *ummatan wasaṭan* as a "just community." However, Abdel Haleem also notes that the literal translation is "a middle nation." Other translators and commentators designate different English terms, such as "middlemost community" or "community of moderation."

In her exploration of the concept of *ummatan wasaṭan*, Asma Afsaruddin suggests that all premodern and modern exegetes hold that *wasaṭ* connotes justice and moderation. Likewise, both the premodern and modern exegetes hold that *ummatan wasaṭan* enacts its particular moderation through both doctrine and praxis, which is to say the middle community is conceived as such because it avoids extremism in belief and in practice.[6]

In his interpretation of this passage, Ṭabarī treats the phrase as describing the middle position between two "extremes." He states: "Neither they [Muslims] are people of extreme [views] in religious matters such as the extreme views of the Christians who took an extreme position as far as celibacy is concerned or what they said about Jesus, nor are they those who were negligent as the Jews who corrupted the book of God, killed their prophets and lied about their lord and disbelieved in him. They [Muslims] are people of the middle and moderation."[7] Having interpreted *wasaṭ* as middle, Ṭabarī provides a large number of narrations to support the meaning of *wasaṭ* as *'adl* (which means "just" or "fair").

Rāzī also follows Ṭabarī's line of thinking. He cites the meaning of *wasaṭ* as the "best" (*wasaṭ* as *khiyār*). This is in line with the verse 3:110, where the term *khayr* is used. Rāzī also provides the meaning of "between the extremes" and refers, like Ṭabarī, to Christians who, according to him, considered Jesus to be a son and a god, and Jews who killed their prophets and distorted their scrip-tures. Rāzī rejects the idea that the entire *ummah* is just, fair, and in the middle, and argues that the Qur'ān was specifically addressing those believers at the time of the revelation of the verse, and those who would come after them who had the attribute of *wasaṭ*.[8]

For Rāzī, the middle or "just" *ummah* has the vocation to "bear witness." Its fundamental purpose is to guide as the Prophet Muhammad has guided, bear-ing witness to the truth, which the prophets communicated in their messages from God and teachings. This is understood to be a reference to what would occur on the Day of Judgment and is specifically connected to the communica-tion of the message of the prophets to their followers, as a testimony from the community of the Prophet Muhammad, being the last of such communities. Although much of the exegetical literature seems to focus on the eschatological dimension of bearing witness, this can easily be used to refer to "bearing wit-ness" in the present world.

The *Ummah* as Understood in the Modern Period

I will now turn to a number of modern interpretations of the purpose and nature of the *ummah* as it is used in the Qur'ān. Each interpretation offers different emphases, which reflect the nature of their respective projects. These commentaries offer further insights into what the purpose of the *ummah* could (or should) be. They are especially useful in thinking about the different ways the *ummah* has been called upon in the service of politics. For this discussion, I will draw mainly on the various interpretations of Q. 2:143.

Moderation and the "Middlemost Community" (*Ummatan Wasaṭan*)

Central to all modern interpretations is the treatment of the term *ummatan wasaṭan*, the translation of which is varied, as I discussed earlier.

First, I will touch on Muhammad Asad's interpretation of "middlemost com-munity." Unlike some of his contemporaries, Asad (a Jewish convert to Islam and a well-known Muslim thinker) does not assign a particularly active purpose to the *ummah* but instead focuses on the key attributes or qualities. He describes the middlemost community as follows:

A community that keeps an equitable balance between extremes and is realistic in its appreciation of man's nature and possibilities, rejecting both licentiousness and exaggerated asceticism. In tune with its oft-repeated call to moderation in every aspect of life, the Qur'ān exhorts the believers not to place too great an emphasis on the physical and material aspects of their lives, but postulates at the same time, that man's urges and desires relating to this "life of the flesh" are God-willed and, therefore, legitimate.[9]

For Asad, moderation occurs in relation to daily life. In this sense, it is not strongly goal driven but rather a moderate self-limitation in relation to consumption, materialism, and interpersonal relations. Nevertheless, in relation to Q. 3:110, Asad does suggest that the *ummah* needs to prepare for struggle. He states: "Our being a worthy *Ummah* in the sight of God depends on our being prepared to struggle, always and under all circumstances, for the upholding of justice and the abolition of injustice: and this should preclude the possibility of a truly Islamic community being unjust to non-Muslims."[10]

Another modern scholar, the founder of Jamaat-i Islami of Pakistan and one of the leading figures of "political Islamism," Abu'l-Ala Mawdudi (d. 1979) is careful to explain how *ummatan wasaṭan* ultimately reflects the multilayered nature and purpose of the *ummah*. He says:

The Arabic expression which we have translated as "the community of the middle way" is too rich in meaning to find an adequate equivalent in any other language. It signifies that distinguished group of people which follows the path of justice and equity, of balance and moderation, a group which occupies a central position amongst the nationals of the world so that its friendship with all is based on righteousness and justice and none receives its support in wrong and injustice.[11]

The *ummah* in the postprophetic world should collectively reenact the practice of the Prophet, thereby "communicating to mankind what the Prophet had communicated to them, or in exemplifying in their own lives what the Prophet had, by his own conduct, translated into actual practice."[12]

This implies a global leadership role for the *ummah*. Mawdudi states: "What it actually means is that just as the Prophet served as living example of godliness and moral rectitude, of equity and fair play before the Muslim community, so is the Muslim community required to stand vis-à-vis the whole world."[13] Although this is a heavy responsibility, it is also—according to Mawdudi—"the highest reward that can be granted to a people in recognition of its righteousness."[14]

Another contemporary scholar, a key figure of Muslim Brotherhood of Egypt, Sayyid Quṭb (d. 1966), offers an interpretation of the meaning of *umma-tan wasaṭan* that is similar to that of Mawdudi. For Quṭb, "the Muslim Ummah is a moderate nation which stands witness against other nations and communities in the sense that it upholds and defends justice and equality for all people."[15] This model for moderation is personified in the Prophet Muhammad, who is the exemplar for those within the *ummah*.[16] Notably, in this conception the *ummah* simultaneously carries a transcendent truth and is sensitive to the context in which this truth is to be communicated. The *ummah* is therefore not rigid or dogmatic but "holds fast to its ideals and tradition, and to the sources of its religion and way of life, while fostering change and progress in all fields."[17]

Ummah and Purpose

These modern-day scholars carefully examine the importance of purpose in relation to the *ummah*. Asad, as discussed earlier, firmly believed the purpose of the *ummah* was to champion justice and fairness, even to the point of violent struggle. For Mawdudi, the purpose of the *ummah* at all stages was made explicit in Surah 2, verse 143, of the Qurʾān. Mawdudi suggests that this verse both outlines the nature of the *ummah* and also reveals the responsibility attributed to it. This responsibility is to carry "on the Prophet's mission, which he had bequeathed to [the *ummah*], in a perfected form on both conceptual and practical levels."[18] More specifically, for Mawdudi, this text of the Qurʾān "constitutes the proclamation appointing the religious community (ummah) consisting of the followers of Muhammad to religious guidance and leadership of the world."[19]

For Mawdudi, active leadership amounts to standing witness.[20] Quṭb interprets the idea of "witness" differently. He argues that the *ummah* must serve as the ultimate example in comparison with "other nations and communities."[21] By this Quṭb means that the *ummah* "upholds and defends justice and equality for all people."[22] For the *ummah* to stand witness, it must pioneer the middle way of the prophet in a worldly and active way, as "a standard-setter" and a "world model for moderation of the social, political and economic ideals, values, traditions and principles it advocates and represents."[23]

Quṭb defines the *ummah* as a group that is inextricably bound through the sharing of the same faith, which then must be collectively enacted.[24] He suggests that in the Meccan period Muslims were not yet a coherent group, and the

Qur'ān was the key tool that allowed the *ummah* to form.[25] This extends to the modern period, as the Qur'ān has given the *ummah* definition such that it is "a community with a well-defined purpose."[26] The purpose of collectively implementing the truth is, for Quṭb, made explicit in Q. 7:181–83: "Among those whom We have created there is a community who guide others by means of the truth and with it establish justice. As for those who deny Our revelations, We will lead them on, step by step, from whence they cannot tell; for although I may give them respite, My subtle scheme is mighty."[27]

Quṭb suggests that the *ummah* is active and dynamic. The *ummah*, according to Quṭb, "are not happy to keep it to themselves, or be inward looking. They try to publicize the truth they know, and guide other people to it."[28] The *ummah* has a leadership role, assuming that if the propagation of truth is enacted properly, then the establishment of justice will follow.[29]

Ummah and Political Transformation

Quṭb's conception of the *ummah* and its purpose is strictly tied to his broader political project, which is a response to the fragmented society. Society has, he states, "abandoned the religion God has chosen for them, and adopted social and political philosophies and systems that are inconsistent with it."[30] The modern world is not being guided by the truth, and the *ummah* is not performing their leadership role. This role, according to Quṭb, must be earned through struggle to "prove its loyalty and dedication to God and show total allegiance to the leadership and legacy of Muhammad, God's Messenger."[31]

Particularly striking in Quṭb's interpretation of the meaning of the *ummah* and its purpose are his ideas about what sacred text and doctrine facilitate. They provide, as Ibrahim Abu-Rabi' explains, "a method of transformation, revolution, and reconstruction."[32] Furthermore, "method awakes the Ummah to its responsibilities, the essence of which is to ponder the 'sea of *jahiliyah*' [akin to pre-Islamic ignorance and lack of faith in God] for the sake of changing it."[33] The *ummah* therefore carries a revolutionary potential, as its purpose is to bring about change in accordance with Qur'ānic truth.

For Quṭb, as Abu-Rabi' explains, the acquisition of power that is needed to establish the Islamic state is contingent on the constitution of a modern *ummah* that can act as a revolutionary vanguard. This *ummah* vanguard "must cut itself off from the modern *jahiliyah*, its norms, and theory of knowledge."[34] For Quṭb, this can only be achieved through a strict adherence to the apparently clear doctrinal message of the Qur'ān. As Abu-Rabiʿ puts it: "The vanguard must go back to the Qur'ān to quench its thirst for knowledge."[35]

Mawdudi also looks back to the time of revelation as the prime example of the "final success of the universal Islamic revolution."[36] He identifies collective belief in the oneness of God as a shared power that can have political implications. This is inextricably tied to the idea "that God intended man to be the *khalifa* (vicegerent) of God."[37] For Mawdudi, vicegerency is critical and a "collective right of all those who accept and admit God's absolute sovereignty over themselves and adopt the divine code, conveyed through the prophet, as the law above all laws."[38] The acquisition of power in order to establish the Islamic state is thus contingent on this collective recognition of God's sovereignty and living according to His way: "Vicegerents are the totality of Muslim believers who submit to the One Sovereign and His laws received through the prophet having repudiated all previous national, ethnic or cultural norms."[39]

Ummah from a Sociological Perspective

Away from the strongly political emphasis on the understanding of *ummah*, Riaz Hassan, a Pakistani-Australian sociologist, looks at the term *ummah* from a sociological perspective. First, alongside the emergence of Islam, Hassan suggests that the "ummah became a transformative concept in the sense that it played a significant role, changing first, the Arab tribes into an Arab community and, later as Islam began to expand to non-Arab lands, different groups of Muslims into a community of believers."[40] This foundational aspect of the *ummah* continues to function in the contemporary context.

A second key aspect unfolded under the leadership of the Rāshidūn caliphs alongside early Muslim expansionism. Here, according to Hassan, the "*ummah* became a framework for maintaining religious unity and accommodating the cultural diversities of the believers. This generated a strong sense of unity, which permeated the Muslim world and was instrumental in submerging, or over-riding, the significant ethnic and cultural differences on the level of the ideal."[41]

A third key aspect is the *ummah*'s functioning in the modern world of nation-states, and also now in the context of globalization. Here the question arises: how does the concept of the *ummah* function in an environment where Muslims are tied to local realities and national boundaries and at the same time increasingly interconnected on a transnational level? Ultimately, Hassan argues "that in Muslim countries, political culture will evolve in response to national aspiration, and not to the ummah's aspirations."[42] Hassan argues that in this context, "the future Islamic ummah will gain strength not as a unified and unitary community but as a differentiated one consisting of ummah that represent different Islamic regions."[43]

Commenting on how *ummah* functions today, Gabriele Marranci, a Muslim anthropologist, argues that "the Ummah becomes visible and 'activated' in its 'trans-ethnic' and 'trans-national' ethos during particular emotional events."[44] This means that "although different forms of sectarianism exist among Muslims, they can be considered as part of an internal dynamic, which, however, does not contradict or deny the shared, and fundamental, basic ethos."[45] Key examples of this are the Rushdie affair and the Danish Cartoon affair, which have generated a collective response in the name of the transnational *ummah* transcending any internal division that undoubtedly exists within and across contemporary Muslim nations.[46]

Conclusion

The classical and modern periods of Qur'ānic interpretation emphasize the community of Prophet Muhammad as the best possible *ummah*, albeit conditional upon maintaining faith in God, ensuring justice and equity among people, commanding good, and forbidding what is evil.

These functions seem straightforward at an abstract level, and the classical commentators did not delve into the practical implications of such concepts. They simply took for granted what the text appears to have said and related their understanding to the application of Qur'ānic and Sunnah norms and values in the community. Their emphasis throughout was on the religious community, and they rarely discussed the political community of Muslims and associated political power.

Although a similar tendency has continued in the modern period, there is now more debate on the purpose of the *ummah* in terms of upholding of justice within an increasingly complex social and political context. The examples covered suggest that the *ummah* is not a fixed notion: but rather a concept that has transformed over time and continues to change as social and political contexts change, as can be seen in the debates among contemporary Muslim commentators and thinkers.

Notes

1. All Qur'an passages are taken from the translation by M. A. S. Abdel Haleem, *The Qur'an* (Oxford: Oxford University Press, 2004).

2. Tabari, *Jami' al-Bayan*, Interpretation of Qur'an 3:110 (Beirut: Dar al-Kutub al-'Ilmiyah, 1997).

3. Rāzī, *al-Tafsir al-Kabir*, Interpretation of Qur'an 3:110.

4. Ibn Kathir, *Tafsir,* Interpretation of Qur'an 3:110.

5. Tabari, Interpretation of Qur'an 3:110.

6. Asma Afsaruddin, "The Hermeneutics of Inter-Faith Relations: Retrieving Moderation and Pluralism as Universal Principles in Qur'anic Exegeses," *Journal of Religious Ethics* 37, no. 2 (2009): 347.

7. Tabari, *Jami' al-Bayan*, Interpretation of Qur'an 2:143.

8. Rāzī, *al-Tafsir al-Kabir,* Interpretation of Qur'an 2:143.

9. Muhammad Asad, *The Message of the Qur'an* (Gibraltar: Dar al-Andalus, 1980). See his commentary on Q. 2:143.

10. Muhammad Asad, *This Law of Ours and Other Essays* (Gibraltar: Dar al-Andalus, 1987), 80.

11. Sayyid Abul A'la Mawdudi, *Towards Understanding the Qur'an*, Vol. I, *Suras 1–3*, trans. Zafar Ishaq Ansari (Leicester: Islamic Foundation, 1988), 121.

12. Ibid.

13. Ibid.

14. Ibid., 126.

15. Sayyid Qutb, *In the Shade of the Qur'ān*, Vol. I, *Surahs 1–2*, translated by Adil Salahi (Leicester: Islamic Foundation, 2002), 137.

16. Ibid.

17. Ibid.

18. Mawdudi, *Towards Understanding the Qur'an*, I:19.

19. Ibid., 120.

20. Ibid., 121.

21. Qutb, *In the Shade of the Qur'ān*, I:137.

22. Ibid.

23. Ibid.

24. Sayyid Qutb, *In the Shade of the Qur'an*, Vol. VI, *Surah 7*, translated by Adil Salahi (Leicester: Islamic Foundation, 2002), 281–82.

25. Ibrahim M. Abu-Rabi', *Intellectual Origins of Islamic Resurgence in the Modern Arab World* (Albany: State University of New York Press, 1996), 173.

26. Qutb, *In the Shade of the Qur'an*, VI:281.

27. Surah 7:181–83 in ibid.

28. Qutb, *In the Shade of the Qur'an*, VI:282.

29. Ibid.

30. Ibid., I:150.

31. Ibid.

32. Abu-Rabi', 188–89.

33. Abu-Rabi', *Intellectual Origins of Islamic Resurgence*, 188–89.

34. Ibid., 185.

35. Ibid.

36. David Emmanuel Singh, "Integrative Political Ideology of Mawlana Mawdudi and Islamisation of the Muslim Masses in the Indian Subcontinent," *South Asia: Journal of South Asian Studies*, 23, no. 1 (2000): 137.

37. Ibid., 131.

38. Mawdudi, cited in ibid., 132.

39. Singh, "Integrative Political Ideology," 132.

40. Riaz Hassan, "Globalisation's Challenge to the Islamic *Ummah*," *Asian Journal of Social Science* 34, no. 2 (2006): 312.

41. Ibid.

42. Ibid., 318.

43. Riaz Hassan, *Faithlines: Muslim Conceptions of Islam and Society* (Pakistan: Oxford University Press, 2002), 112.

44. Gabrielle Marranci, *The Anthropology of Islam* (New York: Berg, 2008), 112.

45. Ibid., 114.

46. The Rushdie Affair refers to the reaction to the publication of Salman Rushdie's novel *The Satanic Verses* in 1988—a reaction including the issuance by Ayatollah Ruhollah Khomeini of Iran of a fatwa calling for Rushdie's death. The Danish Cartoon affair refers to the publication in 2005, first in the Danish newspaper *Jyllands-Posten,* then elsewhere, of a dozen editorial cartoons depicting the Prophet Muhammad in ways deemed offensive by most Muslims, the protest of which turned violent in many parts of the world.

Scripture Dialogue I
God's People Israel and the Church

T he passages from Exodus and 1 Peter have been placed together here because the account of Israel given in the former (especially at v. 6) is quoted at 1 Peter 2:9 ("a royal priesthood, a holy nation").

Exodus 19:1–6

Commentary

This passage occurs at an important moment in the story of the people of Israel. God has recently brought them out of slavery in Egypt, and, led by Moses, they have been brought to Mount Sinai, in the wilderness, where God will establish his covenant with them and give them laws to shape their life as his chosen people. The following chapters of Exodus include the giving of the Ten Commandments and the making of the covenant. As in the earlier story of Abraham, who is called by God to be a blessing to the nations (Genesis 12:1–3), the vocation of Israel here involves both being set apart from other nations but also a role on behalf of the wider world. Israel is a "priestly kingdom," and the function of priests is to make possible God's relationship to others.

Biblical text:

[1]At the third new moon after the Israelites had gone out of the land of Egypt, on that very day, they came into the wilderness of Sinai. [2]They had journeyed from Rephidim, entered the wilderness of Sinai, and camped in the wilderness; Israel camped there in front of the mountain. [3]Then Moses went up to God; the Lord called to him from the mountain, saying, "Thus you shall say to the house of Jacob, and tell the Israelites: [4]You have seen what I did to the Egyptians, and how I bore you on eagles' wings and brought you to myself. [5]Now therefore, if you obey my voice and keep my covenant, you shall be my treasured possession out of all the peoples. Indeed, the whole earth is mine, [6]but you shall be

for me a priestly kingdom and a holy nation. These are the words that you shall speak to the Israelites."

1 Peter 2:9–10

Commentary

The first letter of Peter addresses believers in Jesus Christ, placing great emphasis on the death and resurrection of Jesus as the redemptive acts of the God of Israel. Just as the exodus from Egypt created the redeemed people of Israel, called to live as God's people among the nations of the world, so the death and resurrection of Jesus are now seen as the typological fulfillment of the exodus. Believers in Jesus have been called out of the darkness of sin into God's "marvelous light" and are addressed in terms previously applied to Israel. As well as Exodus 19, Peter also quotes (in v. 10) from the prophet Hosea (2:23); again, the story and the vocation of Israel are being applied to the Church of Jesus Christ.

Biblical text:

⁹But you are a chosen race, a royal priesthood, a holy nation, God's own people, in order that you may proclaim the mighty acts of him who called you out of darkness into his marvelous light.

¹⁰Once you were not a people,
   but now you are God's people;
once you had not received mercy,
   but now you have received mercy.

Romans 11:28–32

Commentary

Whereas the texts from Exodus and 1 Peter can readily be understood as suggesting that the Church "replaces" or "supersedes" Israel, the following passage from Romans 11 is one of the New Testament passages most often cited by those arguing for a different, nonsupersessionist Christian view of Judaism.

Chapters 9–11 of Paul's letter to the early Christian community in Rome are a distinct section of his account of the Christian faith. In chapters 1–8 Paul explains how God's action in the death and resurrection of Jesus and the sending of the Holy Spirit brings salvation to sinful humanity. Then he turns to a question that concerns him deeply: what of those Jews, his kinsfolk, who have not believed in Jesus? (Rom. 9:1–5). The complex argument that follows cannot easily be summarized here, but for our present purposes the key points are that although Paul longs and prays for all his kinsfolk to recognize Jesus as the long-awaited Messiah (10:1), he also warns Gentile Christians not to take an arrogant or dismissive view of Jews who do not believe in Jesus. In the passage below Paul argues that the gifts and call of God (to Israel) are irrevocable and that the outworking of the mercy of God in history will be more mysterious and more inclusive than expected. In this passage, "they" refers to Jews who have not believed in Jesus, while "you" refers to Gentile members of the Christian community in Rome.

Biblical text:

[28]As regards the gospel they are enemies of God for your sake; but as regards election they are beloved, for the sake of their ancestors; [29]for the gifts and the calling of God are irrevocable. [30]Just as you were once disobedient to God but have now received mercy because of their disobedience, [31]so they have now been disobedient in order that, by the mercy shown to you, they too may now receive mercy. [32]For God has imprisoned all in disobedience so that he may be merciful to all.

Scripture Dialogue II
The Umma and Earlier Religious Communities

Qur'ān 2:120–45

Commentary

This key passage, by far the longest selection from the Qur'ān to have been discussed at the 2013 Building Bridges seminar, is relevant not just for Scripture Dialogue II but also for other sessions. It is given here in its entirety in the expectation that we will return to it at various points.

This passage is understood as belonging to the earliest Medinan period, not long after Muhammad and his followers had migrated from Mecca to Medina (the Hijra). This new context brought Muhammad and the Muslim community into contact with the Jewish communities of Medina as well as with some Christians. Verses such as 120 and 135 indicate the lively interreligious encounter that ensued, with the conflicting truth claims of the different communities apparently being openly debated.

From verse 122 the Qur'ān directly addresses the "Children of Israel," moving soon into an account of Abraham, which affirms that the message brought by Muhammad is in continuity with that which was revealed to Abraham and other prophets after him. Key points include:

- Being a physical descendant of Abraham does not automatically place one in a covenant relationship with God, which excludes "wrong-doers." (v. 124)
- Abraham and Ishmael are associated with God's house at Mecca (Makka) (vv. 125–27). They pray that God will raise up from their seed a nation (*umma*) submissive (*muslīma*) to him (v. 128) and that God will raise up for this people a messenger who will recite God's revelations to them (v. 129).
- Abraham calls upon his sons and also Jacob to surrender to God (vv. 131–33), the verb for "surrender" being cognate with *islām* and *muslim*.

Summarizing these points, at verse 136 the Qur'ān calls upon Muhammad's fellow believers to announce that they believe in what God has revealed to them through Muhammad and that this is the same as what God had revealed to earlier communities through messengers from Abraham to Jesus. Those who share this belief are "rightly guided" while those who turn away are "in schism" (v. 137).

The final verses of this selection (142–45) concern the episode known as the "change of *qibla*." The *qibla* (direction of prayer) of Muhammad and the believers had been Jerusalem, but at this early stage in Medina the *qibla* was changed by God to Mecca—a dramatic and very public reorientation marking a significant shift in intercommunal relations. These verses express the divine purpose in the change of *qibla* and, at verse 145, indicate that this development underlines the difference between the Muslim community and "those who have received the Scripture" but have not believed Muhammad's message.

Qur'ānic text:

[120]And the Jews will not be pleased with thee [Muhammad], nor will the Christians, till thou follow their creed. Say: Lo! the guidance of God (Himself) is Guidance. And if thou shouldst follow their desires after the knowledge which hath come unto thee, then wouldst thou have from God no protecting guardian nor helper.

[121]Those unto whom We have given the Scripture, who read it with the right reading, those believe in it. And whoso disbelieveth in it, those are they who are the losers.

[122]O Children of Israel! Remember My favour wherewith I favoured you and how I preferred you to (all) creatures.

[123]And guard (yourselves) against a day when no soul will in aught avail another, nor will compensation be accepted from it, nor will intercession be of use to it; nor will they be helped.

[124]And (remember) when his Lord tried Abraham with (His) commands, and he fulfilled them, He said: Lo! I have appointed thee a leader for mankind. (Abraham) said: And of my offspring (will there be leaders)? He said: My covenant includeth not wrong-doers.

[125]And when We made the House (at Makka) a resort for mankind and sanctuary, (saying): Take as your place of worship the place where Abraham stood (to pray). And We imposed a duty upon Abraham and Ishmael, (saying): Purify

My house for those who go around and those who meditate therein and those who bow down and prostrate themselves (in worship).

126And when Abraham prayed: My Lord! Make this a region of security and bestow upon its people fruits, such of them as believe in God and the Last Day, He answered: As for him who disbelieveth, I shall leave him in contentment for a while, then I shall compel him to the doom of Fire—a hapless journey's end!

127And when Abraham and Ishmael were raising the foundations of the House, (Abraham prayed): Our Lord! Accept from us (this duty). Lo! Thou, only Thou, art the Hearer, the Knower.

128Our Lord! And make us submissive unto Thee and of our seed a nation submissive unto Thee, and show us our ways of worship, and relent toward us. Lo! Thou, only Thou, art the Relenting, the Merciful.

129Our Lord! And raise up in their midst a messenger from among them who shall recite unto them Thy revelations, and shall instruct them in the Scripture and in wisdom and shall make them grow. Lo! Thou, only Thou, art the Mighty, Wise.

130And who forsaketh the religion of Abraham save him who befooleth himself? Verily We chose him in the world, and lo! in the Hereafter he is among the righteous.

131When his Lord said unto him: Surrender! he said: I have surrendered to the Lord of the Worlds.

132The same did Abraham enjoin his sons, and also Jacob, (saying): O my sons! Lo! God hath chosen for you the (true) religion; therefore die not save as men who have surrendered (unto Him).

133Or were ye present when death came to Jacob, when he said unto his sons: What will ye worship after me? They said: We shall worship thy god, the god of thy fathers, Abraham and Ishmael and Isaac, One God, and unto Him we have surrendered.

134Those are a people who have passed away. Theirs is that which they earned, and yours is that which ye earn. And ye will not be asked of what they used to do.

135And say: Be Jews or Christians, then ye will be rightly guided. Say (unto them, O Muhammad): Nay, but (we follow) the religion of Abraham, the upright, and he was not of the idolaters.

136Say (O Muslims): We believe in God and that which is revealed unto us and that which was revealed unto Abraham, and Ishmael, and Isaac, and Jacob, and the tribes, and that which Moses and Jesus received, and that which the prophets received from their Lord. We make no distinction between any of them, and unto Him we have surrendered.

¹³⁷And if they believe in the like of that which ye believe, then are they rightly guided. But if they turn away, then are they in schism, and God will suffice thee (for defense) against them. He is the Hearer, the Knower.

¹³⁸(We take our) colour from God, and who is better than God at colouring. We are His worshippers.

¹³⁹Say (unto the People of the Scripture): Dispute ye with us concerning God when He is our Lord and your Lord? Ours are our works and yours your works. We look to Him alone.

¹⁴⁰Or say ye that Abraham, and Ishmael, and Isaac, and Jacob, and the tribes were Jews or Christians? Say: Do ye know best, or doth God? And who is more unjust than he who hideth a testimony which he hath received from God? God is not unaware of what ye do. ¹⁴¹Those are a people who have passed away; theirs is that which they earned and yours that which ye earn. And ye will not be asked of what they used to do.

¹⁴²The foolish of the people will say: What hath turned them from the qiblah which they formerly observed? Say: Unto God belong the East and the West. He guideth whom He will unto a straight path.

¹⁴³Thus We have appointed you a middle nation, that ye may be witnesses against mankind, and that the messenger may be a witness against you. And We appointed the *qiblah* which ye formerly observed only that We might know him who followeth the messenger, from him who turneth on his heels. In truth it was a hard (test) save for those whom God guided. But it was not God's purpose that your faith should be in vain, for God is Full of Pity, Merciful toward mankind.

¹⁴⁴We have seen the turning of thy face to heaven (for guidance, O Muhammad). And now verily We shall make thee turn (in prayer) toward a qiblah which is dear to thee. So turn thy face toward the Inviolable Place of Worship, and ye (O Muslims), wheresoever ye may be, turn your faces (when ye pray) toward it. Lo! Those who have received the Scripture know that (this revelation) is the Truth from their Lord. And God is not unaware of what they do.

¹⁴⁵And even if thou broughtest unto those who have received the Scripture all kinds of portents, they would not follow thy *qiblah*, nor canst thou be a follower of their qiblah; nor are some of them followers of the *qiblah* of others. And if thou shouldst follow their desires after the knowledge which hath come unto thee, then surely wert thou of the evil-doers.

Qurʾān 3:113–15 and 5:65–66

Commentary

The following two shorter passages come from later in the Medinan period and reflect further dealings between the Muslim community and the "People of the Scripture" (more commonly rendered "People of the Book"), a term that can refer to Jews or Christians or both. The significance of these passages for this session is that they recognize distinctions among the People of the Book; they "are not all alike" (3:113); some are "moderate" while many are "of evil conduct" (5:66). 3:113–15 in particular has warm praise for some among the People of the Book who are characterized in very similar terms to the Muslims. Thus what is said of them at 3:114 repeats what had been said of the Muslims at verse 110 (a text to be studied in Scripture Dialogue IV).

Qurʾān 3:113–15

¹¹³They are not all alike. Of the People of the Scripture there is a staunch community who recite the revelations of God in the night season, falling prostrate (before Him).

¹¹⁴They believe in God and the Last Day, and enjoin right conduct and forbid indecency, and vie one with another in good works. These are of the righteous.

¹¹⁵And whatever good they do, they will not be denied the meed thereof. God is Aware of those who ward off (evil).

Qurʾān 5:65–66

⁶⁵If only the People of the Scripture would believe and ward off (evil), surely We should remit their sins from them and surely We should bring them into Gardens of Delight.

⁶⁶If they had observed the Torah and the Gospel and that which was revealed unto them from their Lord, they would surely have been nourished from above them and from beneath their feet. Among them there are (a) people who are moderate, but many of them are of evil conduct.

Scripture Dialogue III
The Nature and Purpose of the Church

Ephesians 4:1–16

Commentary

Ephesians 4:1 marks a turning point in this letter. In chapters 1–3 Paul has expounded the redemptive action of God through Jesus Christ. Now he turns to how believers should live in the light of this good news, and his essential point is that they are called to live as "the body of Christ." This image of the Church as Christ's body, which occurs only in Paul's writings, is also elaborated at Romans 12 and 1 Corinthians 12. The image implies both unity (a body is one) and diversity (a body has many parts). The Church is thus equipped with diverse ministries, all directed toward the one task of "building up the body of Christ" (v. 12). As members of the body of Christ, Christians are to "grow up" (v. 15), being transformed into the likeness of Christ. The idea of the "body of Christ" is central to a widespread theology of the Church as "the extension of the Incarnation."

Biblical text:

¹I therefore, the prisoner in the Lord, beg you to lead a life worthy of the calling to which you have been called, ²with all humility and gentleness, with patience, bearing with one another in love, ³making every effort to maintain the unity of the Spirit in the bond of peace. ⁴There is one body and one Spirit, just as you were called to the one hope of your calling, ⁵one Lord, one faith, one baptism, ⁶one God and Father of all, who is above all and through all and in all.

⁷But each of us was given grace according to the measure of Christ's gift. ⁸Therefore it is said,

"When he ascended on high he made captivity itself a captive;

he gave gifts to his people."

⁹(When it says, "He ascended," what does it mean but that he had also descended into the lower parts of the earth? ¹⁰He who descended is the same

one who ascended far above all the heavens, so that he might fill all things.) ¹¹The gifts he gave were that some would be apostles, some prophets, some evangelists, some pastors and teachers, ¹²to equip the saints for the work of ministry, for building up the body of Christ, ¹³until all of us come to the unity of the faith and of the knowledge of the Son of God, to maturity, to the measure of the full stature of Christ. ¹⁴We must no longer be children, tossed to and fro and blown about by every wind of doctrine, by people's trickery, by their craftiness in deceitful scheming. ¹⁵ But speaking the truth in love, we must grow up in every way into him who is the head, into Christ, ¹⁶from whom the whole body, joined and knitted together by every ligament with which it is equipped, as each part is working properly, promotes the body's growth in building itself up in love.

Matthew 28:16–20

Commentary

This passage (sometimes known as "The Great Commission") is a key New Testament text expressing the outward orientation of the Church, its purpose in the wider world. In these verses, which conclude Matthew's Gospel, the risen Jesus commissions the disciples to make disciples of all nations, baptizing them and instructing them in his teaching.

Biblical text:

¹⁶Now the eleven disciples went to Galilee, to the mountain to which Jesus had directed them. ¹⁷When they saw him, they worshipped him; but some doubted. ¹⁸And Jesus came and said to them, "All authority in heaven and on earth has been given to me. ¹⁹Go therefore and make disciples of all nations, baptizing them in the name of the Father and of the Son and of the Holy Spirit, ²⁰and teaching them to obey everything that I have commanded you. And remember, I am with you always, to the end of the age."

Scripture Dialogue IV
The Nature and Purpose of the Umma

Qurʾān 2:143

Commentary

See Scripture Dialogue I commentary on 2:120–45 for the general context of this verse. The first part of 2:143 is of particular interest for this session on the nature and purpose of the *umma*. The believing community has been appointed "a middle nation" (*ummatan wasaṭan*), to be "witnesses against mankind." (Other translations prefer "over," "before," or "to" rather than "against").

Qurʾānic text:

Thus We have appointed you a middle nation, that ye may be witnesses against mankind, and that the messenger may be a witness against you. And We appointed the *qiblah* which ye formerly observed only that We might know him who followeth the messenger, from him who turneth on his heels. In truth it was a hard (test) save for those whom God guided. But it was not God's purpose that your faith should be in vain, for God is Full of Pity, Merciful toward mankind.

Qurʾān 3:110

Commentary

This is another Medinan passage. The negative comments in the second part of this verse on the majority of the People of the Book throw into relief the statement made in the first part about the excellence and the purpose of the Muslim community, whose task in the world is here expressed in terms of the giving of moral guidance regarding both the good that is to be done and the evil that is to be avoided. The Arabic expression *al-amr b'il ma'rūf wa al-nahy 'an al-munkar* (sometimes translated "commanding right and forbidding wrong"), derived from this and similar Qur'ānic verses, has become the basis of much Islamic writing on the application of this duty.

Qur'ānic text:

Ye are the best community that hath been raised up for mankind. Ye enjoin right conduct and forbid indecency; and ye believe in God. And if the People of the Scripture had believed it had been better for them. Some of them are believers; but most of them are evil-livers.

Qur'ān 5:48

Commentary

This Medinan passage reveals the divine purpose underlying the diversity of *ummas*, and the injunction to use this diversity as a cause not of division but of reciprocal spiritual and moral stimulus. It also underscores the aspect of continuity between the Qur'ānic scripture and all scriptures preceding it: *musaddiq*, confirmer; *muhaymin*, protector ("watcher," in the translation below). Insofar as the community is formed by its scripture, the implication is that the Muslim *umma* must see itself as a confirmer and protector of all preceding it.

Qur'ānic text:

And unto the [Muhammad] have We revealed the Scripture with the truth, confirming whatever Scripture was before it, and a final authority over it. So judge between them by that which God hath revealed, and follow not their desires away from the truth which hath come unto thee. For each We have appointed a divine law and a traced-out way. Had God willed He could have made you one *Umma*. But that He may try you by that which He hath given you (He hath made you as ye are). So vie one with another in good works. Unto God ye will all return, and He will then inform you of that wherein ye differ.

PART II

Unity and Disunity in the Life of the Community

Perspectives on Christian Desires for Communion and Experiences of Division (or, The History of the Church in Half a Chapter!)

LUCY GARDNER

The topic for this lecture is daunting: the attempt to present a simple account of human lives over a significant amount of time seems worryingly hubristic and will inevitably do violence to their complexity, particularity, and pain. There will be other Christians who would want and need to tell this brief account of Christian history very differently; moreover, this account also bears on Muslim prehistory and self-understandings that would also want to tell the tale differently. I am nevertheless encouraged in the task first by the conviction that, alongside the close reading of texts with each other, we need to listen to each other telling our histories of ourselves and of each other in order to understand one another better; and, second, by the hope that this will enable us to face not only the past but the present and the future together.

Almost every Christian regularly confesses belief in "one, holy, catholic and apostolic Church."[1] These four "notes" or "marks" that characterize the Church and her self-understanding are not entirely separate characteristics. In their proper relations, they are interdependent aspects of each other: in an important sense the Church's unity consists precisely in her being called and separated out by God (holy), to gather together with Christ (God) as her center (in Word and Sacrament) and thus participate in God's holiness, but also in her being sent by that same God (as Christ was/is sent from God, and as the apostles were the sent ones), to join in God's mission to save the whole world (the catholicity of salvation) and to share that holiness and the communion in which it consists with everyone.[2] Being thus called, gathered, and sent is what it means to be the Church. At the same time, of course, the experience of every Christian today is that the Church is palpably not in any ordinary sense "one"; these different aspects exist in tension and cause not so much unity as division. In the face of our divisions, however, one thing that at times nevertheless almost

45

perversely unites many (if not all) Christians is the persistent belief that the Church—we—*should* be united.[3] The fact that we are not is more than regrettable: it is in many senses a scandal.

"Unity and Disunity" is, then, at once an intriguing and a painful theme. In what follows, I attempt a reflection on different approaches to our unity, and different interpretations of these four marks of the Church—in particular, the nature, demands, expression, and tests of and for apostolicity—in considering some New Testament visions of unity and responses to division, some examples of early debates and causes for division, two significant splinterings of the Church in subsequent centuries, and some more recent attempts to heal some of our divisions.[4] It is my hope that amid these oversimplifications some common themes and helpful differentiations can be drawn that will give some sense of the types of unity Christians long for, the sorts of things that they divide over, and the different ways in which they respond to those divisions; and that these in turn might provide some orientations for our work together.

New Testament Visions of Unity and Responses to Division

Why is division in the Church a scandal? Christ's own teaching and that of his apostles is clear. On the night before he died, at the Last Supper, which Christians recall at every celebration of the Eucharist, Christ places loving unity at the heart of his parting instructions for the new community that will grow out of his death and resurrection: "A new commandment I give to you, that you love one another; even as I have loved you. . . . By this all will know that you are my disciples, if you have love for one another" (John 13:34–35).[5] Shortly after this, John records Christ's prayer to the Father for his disciples and those who will follow them; his words (which form one of our texts for study at this seminar) include petitions for their unity, that they may all be one, even as Jesus and the Father are one:

> Holy Father, keep them in thy name, which thou hast given me, that they may be one, even as we are one. . . . I do not pray for these only, but also for those who believe in me through their word, that they may all be one; even as thou, Father, art in me, and I in thee, that they also may be in us. . . . The glory which thou hast given me I have given to them, that they may be one even as we are one, I in them and thou in me, that they may become perfectly one." (John 17:11b–26)[6]

The implications are unmistakable: to belong to Christ is to live in this loving unity and to show it to the world; to fail to do so must directly threaten and undermine all and any attempts at Christian witness together with any claims to belong to Christ or his Church.

For these reasons, the apostles frequently chastise the young churches for which they are responsible, warning them away from the dangers of jealousy, rivalry, bickering, and division. St. Paul has heard that the Corinthians, for example, are dividing themselves according to belonging to different apostles, instead of all asserting that they belong to Christ (1 Cor. 3); that they are pursuing each other for their grievances in the courts, instead of seeking reconciliation (1 Cor. 6); that they are dividing over food offered to idols (1 Cor. 8). Even as they gather as the Church to celebrate the Lord's Supper (or Eucharist) together, they are divided and fail to behave as one body; they neither properly discern nor properly belong to Christ's body and blood that is offered them in that meal, and thereby call down not blessing but condemnation upon themselves (1 Cor. 11:17–33). These links between Christ, his body, the Church, love, and the Eucharist are explored by St. Paul many times.[7] But the theme of the interweaving of uniting love between the Father and the Son, between Christ and the disciples, between the disciples and Christ, between the disciples and each other, of God for the world and of the Church for the world (interrelations that reverberate through the dual command to love God and neighbor) are perhaps most memorably presented for our contemplation in the first letter of St. John:

> Beloved, let us love one another; for love is of God, and he who loves is born of God and knows God. He who does not love does not know God for God is love. In this the love of God was made manifest among us, that God sent his only Son into the world, so that we might live through him. In this is love, not that we loved God but that he loved us and sent his Son to be the expiation for our sins. Beloved, if God so loved us, we also ought to love one another. No one has ever seen God; if we love one another, God abides in us and his love is perfected in us. By this we know that we abide in him and he in us, because he has given us of his own Spirit. And we have seen and testify that the Father has sent his Son as the Saviour of the world. Whoever confesses that Jesus is the Son of God, God abides in him, and he in God. So we know and believe the love God has for us. God is love, and he who abides in love abides in God, and God abides in him. . . . We love because he first loved us. If anyone says "I love God" and hates his brother, he is a liar; for he who does not love his brother whom he has seen cannot love

God whom he has not seen. And this commandment we have from him, that he who loves God should love his brother also. (1 John 4:7–21)

Many of the New Testament texts are letters that seem to have been written, in part at least, in response to experiences of division between and within young Church communities; they represent the apostles, early Christian leaders and teachers, (re)calling fairly recent converts to (greater) unity in Christ and all that entails; combining pastoral encouragement with sometimes patient and sometimes more passionate instruction as to the connections between the content of believing in Jesus and the requirements of following him.

Another early response to division is given in the Acts of the Apostles, chapter 15.[8] Some Jewish Christians were insisting that converts to Jesus Christ needed to be circumcised and exhorted to keep the whole of the (Jewish) law; others were adamant that in Jesus a new dispensation had begun which fulfilled the old law but thus relativized some of it: the new inheritors of Israel did not need to become Jews in order to belong. An assembly of the apostles and representatives from different churches and parties was gathered in Jerusalem to consider the dispute under the guidance of the Holy Spirit. After careful deliberation, a common mind was reached, that it was not necessary for Gentiles to receive circumcision as well as baptism in order to be saved by the Lord Jesus, and this was reported back to the various congregations.[9]

From the New Testament writings, then, it is clear that the early Christians considered unity within and between Christian communities or local churches as not merely desirable but necessary.[10] Its origin, for St. Paul as much as for St. John, is in Christ and in the unity he shares with the Father in the power of the Spirit; its character is of a uniting love which relativizes differences but does not eradicate them.[11] This unity is to be lived out in loving communion, for which the community is dependent on grace, but for which it must also take some responsibility. It also consists in common purpose and a single end: to proclaim the Gospel to the whole world and to bring in all the nations to share an everlasting, holy communion with God. This unity, therefore, reaches out to bring in and include ever greater diversity in one communion. As both the day of Pentecost, when many different people hear the Gospel in their own language, and the disputes over the relationships to Jewish practices show, this unity does not require uniformity.[12] Thus, another aspect of this unity is its universalism (or its "catholicity"): its logic is that it comes from the one God, for the one world that God has made and loves. The unity envisaged by the first Christians thus clearly reflects the four marks of the Church.

There is also another important aspect of the unity of communion set forth in the New Testament. Since it is properly the unity and communion of the whole world having been transformed and even re-created, it will always be "not yet." The community of the Church is itself not fully extant, for the fullness that is offered, as it is required, will only come into being at the Last Day: the unity of the Church has an irreducibly eschatological dimension.[13]

Commitment to unity of this nature will, however, almost inevitably (if somewhat perversely) lead to dispute and division: Which differences are to be relativized? How? Which are to be eradicated? How is acceptable diversity to be accommodated? How are other differences to be resolved? How is unity to be understood between different points in time? And how is it to be realized over geographical distance in different "local" expressions of faith? In the New Testament, we see apostles and teachers reasoning and wrestling with scripture;[14] recalling Christ's actions and words; considering early preaching, together with shared experiences of prayer, mission, and miracles; and seeking the authority of appointed leaders and the guidance of the Holy Spirit as they try to address the divisions and disunity that threaten to give the lie to the Gospel that they seek to proclaim and by which they seek to live in witness to the salvation offered in Jesus Christ.

Debate and Division within the Early Church: The Efforts to Preserve Unity

Unsurprisingly, the inheritors of the apostles continued to experience conflicts.[15] Interpreting these today is an inherently fraught exercise but one that cannot be avoided and must be risked repeatedly. These have often been understood and taught as differences about particular doctrines, particularly of the Incarnation and Trinity. They were, however, of course, always also differences about ecclesiology and self-understanding, reflections on how those four marks were to be understood and expressed, and how such judgments and decisions were to be made, by whom.[16] We are often dependent on official versions and the texts of the "victors" (those whose orthodoxy was gradually asserted over various teachings that were gradually declared as heresy); the views and arguments of others have to be reconstructed from the opposition to them, itself often recorded through the lens of later events and decisions.[17] It is also important to bear in mind that heresy particularly threatens unity when it is in fact an adherence to and a defense of (only) part of the truth; the greater the vehemence, and the greater the approximation to truth, the greater the attraction and so the greater the threat. It is also important to acknowledge that the battles experienced by and within the early Christian churches are inextricably linked to the political and cultural battles of the world within which they found themselves. We cannot attribute any event exclusively to internal or external concerns and forces, nor simply to geographical, or theological, or pastoral considerations.

In the controversy surrounding Montanism for example, the issues of authority, apostolicity, holiness, and therefore unity are very evident.[18] The ecstatic, spiritual experiences of some new prophets directly challenged the emerging ministerial hierarchy, claiming direct, independent inspiration of the Holy Spirit, adding new teaching to Christ's, and envisaging the Church as a small community of the pure and holy, with a very strict moral code.[19] This "movement" was a local church, seeking the authority and guidance of the Holy Spirit, yearning fully to express the Church's call to holiness and to interpret Christ's teaching faithfully in their situation. The wider Church gathered together to reject these new teachings and their additional demands, insisting on adherence to the faith taught by the apostles, as taught by the apostles, and asserting reliance on the authority of the bishops as the overseers and guarantors of adherence to that faith. In this, apostolicity, faithfulness to Jesus, was understood to be both faithfulness to the faith as taught by the apostles, and faithfulness (or loyalty and obedience) to the ministers and ministerial structure for ensuring it.[20]

In the debate with Marcionism, the point of conflict was again one of authority, this time in terms of the relationships of the Jewish Scriptures to the New Covenant.[21] Apparently taking their cue from a simplification of St Paul's complex exposition of the relationships between grace and law, Marcionites claimed that the New Testament contradicted and superseded Jewish Scriptures. The response of local churches and the wider Church was to expel those who supported these views, but the movement was strong enough to form small, strong, enduring, separate communities. One result of the protracted disagreement, however, was to secure firmly the importance of Jewish Scriptures for the Christian and ultimately their place as the Old Testament in the Bible. Apostolicity, faithfulness to Jesus and the apostles, included faithfulness to the scriptures to which he himself and his first followers were faithful, and by which he (and they) understood and explained himself and his significance.

In Arianism, the focus of disagreement was more explicitly Christological, and in particular the appropriate exposition of Jesus as the Son of God.[22] This movement was understood to deny Christ's full divinity; its followers could not accept the expression *homoousios* (of one substance) to describe the relationship between the Son and the Father because they felt it lessened (or at least threatened) the singularity of God.[23] This debate was less of a challenge from a fringe sect or a particular local church but was a full-blown central controversy, reverberating across a growing refraction of the Church (theologically, culturally, and politically) into East and West, with bishops opposing each other and garnering the support of rival and successive emperors. At its best, the debate was about how to be faithful, to scripture and Christian experience, and in particular the sense that it is Jesus who saves (a task of which only God is capable), in words acceptable to all, that made sense in and to the very different philosophical outlooks and vocabularies of the Church's different members, and indeed of the different communities to which she was called to preach.[24] Apostolicity was a question of the right words with the right explanations, drawing on an appropriate philosophy. At its worst, however, this was a violent, traumatic brawl for power.

Mere assertion and counter assertion in free-range theopolitical debate failed to reach consensus on matters of dispute. Inspired by the example of the Apostles in Acts 15, an Ecumenical Council was called at Nicaea in 325 CE by Emperor Constantine. From the theological-ecclesial point of view, the Church's leaders (primarily the bishops) gathered with the common purpose of coming to a common mind on particular issues.[25] A creed (including the disputed term and clearly excluding a range of Christological heresies) was drafted, and the bishops were required to sign it. From the imperial-political point of view, the Council was a means of establishing (or maintaining) peace and good order, including clear borders; those who were excommunicated for contradicting the agreements were also exiled. This exaggerated rather than ameliorated geographical difference and edged the Church toward more formal division. Apostolicity was beginning to be understood not merely in terms of the right words and the right authority but also in terms of belonging to the right bishops and the right ecclesial community (as opposed to others) and standing in right relationship to the surrounding world and culture.[26]

Thus we see in the early debates and divisions of the Church different centers of Christian teaching and different sections of Christian organization in conflict with each other over a variety of interlocking topics, including the content of the Christian faith, the proper structure and conduct of Christian communities, their relationships to each other, and the appropriate locations and mechanisms of authority for deciding on these differences. One common theme to all the disputes, however, is that they all also inevitably touch the heart of Christianity, particularly what is "necessary for salvation," from two perspectives: first, what must be the case for the salvation offered in Jesus Christ to be real, or how can "Jesus saves" be true? And second, how are we to respond to that offer of salvation, or what must people do to be saved? Questions of ecclesial identity were in no way secondary to these.

A traditional account of this history is of the triumph of truth over heresy in which all battles are reduced to a simple version of this one. Another increasingly common, powerful reading of it is as the emergence of a powerful, authoritarian, mainstream, hierarchical center that gradually expelled all challenges, claiming center ground and orthodoxy for itself by violently excluding others. Another (perhaps more nuanced) reading looks at a community struggling with itself, trying to come to terms with who it is and what it stands for, only gradually gaining self-understanding through dispossession and rejection of idealized versions of claims that proved to offer only false hope or partial understanding. All these readings reflect on the Church exploring the true nature of the Church's apostolicity, holiness, catholicity, and unity, and on any of these readings the result was clearly unity won at the price of division; as common mind and common purpose are established among some, others are excluded, often ultimately along geographical lines, as different versions of Christianity take hold—some to die off as sects or become completely different religions, others to persist as somewhat separate, autonomous, heterodox ("pre-Nicene," "pre-Chalcedonian," "Nestorian," or "Monophysite") churches, particularly in the East, fed by cultural and linguistic difference alongside geographical location.[27]

Later Divisions: The Multiplication of Churches

The formal separation of the Eastern and Western churches from each other (roughly along the lines of the division between the Roman and Byzantine administrations) is usually dated to The Great Schism of 1054 and resulted in two rather different ecclesial communities: the Roman Catholic Church in the West, united as a single Latin administration under the Pope in Rome, and the Eastern Orthodox Church in the East, conceived as a group of local, territorial (but not simply "ethnic" or "national") sister churches who originally kept Greek as their liturgical and theological language, united under the Patriarch of Constantinople.[28] Each regarded itself as the one, holy, catholic, apostolic Church reaching back to the day of Pentecost.[29] The "straw that broke the camel's back" was what the East saw as the West's unilateral decision to add the term *filioque* (and from the Son) to the description of the procession of the Spirit from the Father in the ecumenically agreed Nicene creed; the East did not recognize the West's right to do this,[30] nor was the East happy to accept it, because it felt this term misrepresented Trinitarian relations.[31] Living in different worlds and different cultures with significantly irreconcilable vocabularies, the "two lungs" of the one ancient Church, however, had been growing apart for hundreds of years before that, as our brief glance at some early disputes intimates.[32] Again, geography and culture combined with disagreements over the language of theology and the nature of ecclesial authority, both to enrich the Church's tradition, and to weaken her temporal expression: that which unites also divides, as some are held together by the expulsion of others (just as, of course, the division and mutual counter-self-definition between the resulting separate communities is in a sense part of what in fact unites them).

To offer some hopelessly crass generalizations about how the resulting two great churches understand themselves and their instantiation of the marks of the Church: In the Orthodox Church, apostolicity appears to be understood primarily as adherence to the ancient faith in the ancient words, particularly in the ancient liturgy; orthodoxy is as much about worshipping aright as about believing or even behaving aright (these latter will follow from the former). Holiness is a great gift offered to the Church, for her to guard and to share. This happens primarily in the liturgy, at which the whole community shares in and anticipates the eternal, heavenly praise of God, which is the eternal Liturgy; individuals grow in holiness as this participation touches their lives, and by participating in it. Unity is also understood primarily liturgically, and subsequently as consisting in and best expressed as forming a fellowship or family of separate churches united by God in sacramental liturgy and in their shared participation in and anticipation of the heavenly liturgy, and therefore also united in belief, practice, and purpose but juridically and administratively distinct. In the Roman Catholic Church, apostolicity has generally been understood as submission to the primacy of the bishop of Rome (the pope):[33] right belief and right dogma, followed by right behavior, including right liturgy, flow from and are expressed in and as a right relationship to the Church, and to the pope in particular. Holiness is again a gift to the Church, but it consists not so much in the liturgy itself as a whole as in the sacraments at its center, of which the Church is guardian (and in some sense arbiter as well as administrator); communities are sanctified by celebrating these sacraments, and individuals may grow in holiness by receiving them devoutly. Catholicity and unity are understood in terms of each other, and particularly in terms of the pope's (asserted) universal jurisdiction and oversight of a single administration for the whole Church.

One reading of the division between East and West is that the East rejected certain developments in the West. The debates of the Reformation likewise focused on whether certain developments and trajectories within the Western, or Roman Catholic, Church were legitimate.[34] As their name suggests, the Reformers did not set out to start new churches but to reform the one in which they lived; they were protesters not original schismatics.[35] Their concerns were many and complex.[36] In particular, the Reformers felt that the Church had become overconfident in its own works as the means to salvation and holiness; their protest slogans were "*sola scriptura*" (only scripture is authoritative) and "justification by faith" (not by works).[37] Faith was understood to be the quality and fervor of a reliance on and relationship with God in Christ and not merely the acceptance of or obedience to particular ecclesial doctrines and dogmas. The (rest of the) Church was quick to respond to the Reformers' demands, not often in the sense of attending to their areas of concern but rather in the sense of attempting to squash rebellion, challenging them either to tow the party line or to leave (or be expelled).[38] This response compounded the problem, since it appeared to be precisely the type of human, sinful misuse of "spiritual" power in the temporal domain to which Reformers were objecting. It also formalized division, since the Reformers thus found themselves to be Christians "outside the (Roman Catholic) Church" and in need of forming new congregations, which became new churches.

In these new communities, apostolicity was generally construed as faithfulness in terms of a spiritual attachment to Christ, and in terms of commitment to an original or primitive biblical expression of this commitment and its consequences, both in individual lives and in Church order. Holiness was no longer understood primarily in liturgical or ecclesiological terms but rather as a certain personal piety that included a moral rectitude and purity—a pattern of life that rejected sloth, indulgence, and other vices (particularly those of the "flesh") and that dedicated itself instead to Christ's teachings with religious zeal and fervor. Unity was understood not in institutional or organizational terms but in being a community of believers, sharing commitment to Christ and to the Bible, and therefore sharing the purpose of proclaiming the Gospel and converting the world from its wickedness.[39] The traditional three-fold order of bishop, priest, and deacon as the leadership of the Church was largely rejected; local churches were led by a group of locally elected elders who in turn appointed ministers, some of whom might be elected to oversight (superintendents or moderators, not bishops). Their task and authority was not linked to sacrament and mediation but rather was construed as biblical preaching and strict moral teaching. The Church (ideally) was to be seen and understood in the work of the Spirit in relatively free, self-governing local communities or congregational churches, and not at all identified with visible human institutions. In Protestant-ism, therefore, the Church as a whole is either in some sense invisible, or only ever to be partially seen in different local expressions, or perhaps more eschato-logically to be waited and longed for as the coming of the Kingdom. Despite several amalgamations between once separate churches, Protestantism is not "a" church: both its arrival and its continued existence can be seen to represent a seemingly unstoppable multiplication of churches.[40]

The Ecumenical Century: Late Modern Desires for Reconciliation and Visible Unity

After centuries of division and sometimes rancor, the twentieth century saw a remarkable surge of Christian desire for increased, visible unity between Chris-tians and the churches to which they belong. For example, with the eventual foundation of the World Council of Churches in 1948, a body was formed that understood itself not as *a* Church, nor as *the* Church, but as which would come to understand itself as "a fellowship of churches which confess the Lord Jesus Christ as God and Saviour according to the scriptures and therefore seek to fulfil together their common calling to the glory of the one God, Father, Son and Holy Spirit."[41] By 1964, in documents from Vatican II (if not before), the Roman Catholic Church recognized members of other churches as Christians, or separated brethren, even though their churches could not be seen as full expressions of the Church. In 1965 Pope Paul VI and Athenagoras, the patriarch of Constantinople, declared an annulment of their centuries-old reciprocal sen-tences of excommunication, thus taking important steps in healing old wounds and removing obstacles to greater cooperation and the establishment of new forms of unity.[42] Different churches, different groups, and different movements, though, still envisage that unity very differently precisely because they understand the Church and her marks differently. The (perhaps naïve) hopes of many in search of full, visible unity have not (yet) been realized.

As even this hopelessly brief account has shown, the divisions in the Church and between the churches are complex, born of many types of difference, on many different levels and issues, and so the search for unity is likewise complex. Some look primarily for theological convergence; some look for greater sharing of administration; others look for greater trust and independence between separate churches or merely the cessation of hostilities; some are more concerned for the recognition of unity of purpose and shared social engagement on issues of justice, locally and more globally; some look for sacramental reunion or more spiritual union. The "gains" have been real, and several, but the way forward is neither clear nor easy.[43] The demand for penance and repentance for our divisions is surely unavoidable, but this need not be cause for pessimism or paralysis. If nothing else, the twentieth century has shown that certain types and degrees of unity, particularly in new projects, can be found and formed despite stubbornly persistent divisions.

Concluding Reflections on the Quizzical Character of Christian Unity (Postmodern Reimaging of Unity?)

At their best, the twentieth century hopes for greater visible unity among Christians and attempts at reunion between the churches were about the rediscovery of unity as something (to be) received rather than achieved. They were attempts to recover more fully the unity envisioned in the New Testament, as a participation in God's triune unity, granted as a gift from God in our relationship with Christ and by the power of the Spirit. The first letter of Clement declares, "Love knows no schism" (1 Clem. 49:5), and this motto must continue to guide Christians in their search for unity. At the same time, we have had to come to terms with the fact that we understand, express, and receive this unity differently, and that sacraments, worship, beliefs, doctrines, authority, structure, mission, and pastoral care are bound up differently with each other in different churches. We can neither hope to match these up to each other quickly, nor too quickly to unpick them and start again. Real barriers to union (and therefore to our salvation, as to our ability to preach or bring salvation to others) persist.

Rather, perhaps we need to learn more of the ways in which we need each other: we each need each other in order to become one in Christ; we each need each other in order the better to understand the unity, which is not a simple singularity, that we are called to share and exhibit.[44] We still need to learn from Christ (and from each other) about the ways in which unity, catholicity, holiness, and apostolicity do not compete with each other but co-inhere together. In place of conflicting views of apostolicity (and therefore unity) as being faithful to the faith once delivered in terms of expressing the same faith in the same words, *or* expressing the same faith in different words, *or* in terms of loyalty to the (right / the same) bishops; instead of trying to decide whether to make holiness the measure of faithfulness, *or* fervor of faith the measure of holiness; instead of trying to discover the correct algorithm for the relationships between submission to a central jurisdiction and legitimate local autonomy; instead of all this, perhaps we need to work at relearning that our apostolicity consists in being sent, our holiness is from Christ, our catholicity is about being for the world (not about church politics), and our unity exists precisely in and as this being called, gathered, and sent by Christ, and not as something "additional." It should not perhaps surprise us, however, that those things which, in the perfection of the divinity belong and subsist together, tend to pull apart in temporal imperfection and become fractious in the realm of sin.

At the same time, however, we need also to learn the proper place of brokenness in the unity we seek. Christians are, and will only ever be, one "in Christ"; but to receive that unity, we must as communities and as individuals die with him. We need to discover—learn how to receive—our identity as his resurrected but still wounded body; we need to learn to live in the unity that both persists in disunity as it also overcomes disunity, just as it did at the Last Supper, in the garden of Gethsemane, in the abandonment of the cross, and in the disciples' dispersal—both at the crucifixion and again, so differently, at Pentecost. The Church, after all, always exists and acts as and in a certain self-contradiction.[45] And as Christians learn more about our ecclesial unity in Christ, we hope we shall also learn more about the true nature of that unity's apostolicity (its faithfulness to being sent) and its catholicity (its being sent to and for the whole world), and thus also the holy unity that God longs to be shared among all peoples, including, no doubt, between people of different faiths.

Notes

1. The phrase occurs in one of the most widely used Christian creeds, the so-called Nicene Creed (called the "Nicene-Constantinopolitan Creed" by Orthodox Christians),

adopted at the Council of Nicaea in 325 and modified at the Council of Constantinople in 381.

2. Thus, two apparently contradictory tendencies of Church understanding that Gavin D'Costa identifies in his essay included in this volume can be understood as the two sides of this being-sent-as-we-are-gathered while being-gathered-by-being-sent. Church identity, then, is neither fragile nor static but rather sinuous and dynamic; it also very much reflects the pattern of Christ's calling and sending of the very first disciples.

3. That is, if we are not in fact already one, despite so many appearances to the contrary—in which case the question is one of learning to recognize, celebrate, and express that unity appropriately and in its greatest possible fullness.

4. Another gloss on this project is that it is to think about the nature of authority in the Church; this could also be pursued through reflection on the image of the Church as Christ's body, considering the different ways in which our membership of that body and Christ's headship of it have been conceived and expressed.

5. For the avoidance of doubt, the message is repeated—or, rather, it is continued—at John 15:12–17: "This is my commandment, that you love one another as I have loved you. Greater love has no man than this, that a man lay down his life for his friends. You are my friends if you do what I command you. . . . This I command you, to love one another."

6. One of our set texts is taken from this passage.

7. For example, he writes to the Romans, "I bid everyone among you not to think of yourself more highly than you ought. . . . For as in one body we have many members, and all members do not have the same function, so we, though many, are one body in Christ, and individually members of one another. . . . Let love be genuine; hate what is evil, hold fast to what is good; love one another with brotherly affection; outdo one another in showing honour. . . . Live in harmony with one another. . . . If possible, so far as it depends upon you, live peaceably with all. . . . Do not be overcome by evil but overcome evil with good" (Rom. 12:3–21).

8. Another of our set texts is taken from this passage.

9. Despite the clarity of the decision, however, it appears that the debate continued to disturb Christian communities since Paul tackles the question in his letter to the Galatians, which was probably written a few years later.

10. It is because of unity's high importance and desires to preserve it that excommunication (itself an act of separation, excluding someone from [full] membership of the Church, and, later, in particular from participation in the sacraments) is presented as occasionally necessary, in cases of extreme unfaithfulness, and particularly in the face of recalcitrance and refusal of reconciliation. See, for example, Matthew 18:15–18; Romans 16; 1 Corinthians 5. At the same time, the Church has often understood excommunication not as "being thrown out by the authorities" but rather as the authorities declaring that someone has, by their persistent actions and attitudes, placed themselves outside of (full) communion. Moreover, it might be understood as a protection to "exclude" someone from the Eucharist if their attendance would be to call down judgment instead of blessings upon themselves.

11. See, for example, Philippians 2:1–5: "So, if there is any encouragement in Christ, any incentive of love, any participation in the Spirit, any affection and sympathy, complete my joy by being of the same mind, having the same love, being in full accord and of one mind. Do nothing from selfishness or conceit, but in humility count others better than yourselves. . . . Have this mind amongst yourselves which is yours in Christ Jesus."

12. Jews can remain Jews, Gentiles remain in some sense Gentiles, while in another sense none of these differences matters: "For as many of you as were baptized into Christ have put on Christ. There is neither Jew nor Greek, neither slave nor free; there is neither male nor female; for you are all one in Christ Jesus. And if you are Christ's, then you are Abraham's offspring, heirs according to the promise" (Gal. 3:27–29).

13. This is particularly richly and enigmatically portrayed in the book of the Revelation to St. John. The Last Day itself, then, will be an act of God, not of the Church. Although not strictly, or simply "of the Church," however, this event will concern the Church; it will be its full realization, its consummation, its end; but it will therefore in some sense also be its ending: the Church's role or function will cease to be to preach the Gospel to the nations, to serve God's world, to be Christ's presence in and to the world, but rather become merely that of contemplating and praising God (within the structure of the Trinity itself: praising the Father, in and through the Son, and in the power of the Spirit), in the new world, forever. It is an occasion which, very vividly for Christians of the New Testament, might be tomorrow, and for Christians today might still be tomorrow—or thousands of years hence. Even in the light of our divisions, "the church must regard waiting as the most creative of activities, since she apprehends fullness of being only in the coming of the Kingdom. And God may act tomorrow. . . . Theology is itself a form of the waiting we must practice." Robert Jenson, *Systematic Theology*, Vol. 1, *The Triune God* (Oxford: Oxford University Press, 2001), viii.

14. "Scripture" here is mostly the Jewish writings, which later came to be called the Old Testament.

15. J. N. D. Kelly's *Early Christian Creeds* (London: A&C Black, 1950) and *Early Christian Doctrines* (London: A&C Black, 1958) provide useful "classic" accounts of these debates; a more recent (and more easily readable) account of them as they relate to the doctrine of the Trinity is given by Franz Dünzl in his *A Brief History of the Doctrine of the Trinity in the Early Church* (Edinburgh: T&T Clark, 2007).

16. The same is true today. Many contested issues within the Church are also contests about authority. For example, some in the Church of England who feel unable to accept any priestly ministry from women do not think that women cannot or should not be priests; rather, they do not believe that the Church of England (or even the Anglican Communion) can or should decide to make such a change to Church order apart from the wider Church of which they understand her to be a legitimate part.

17. And of course some individuals became associated with condemned teachings and practices that were not in fact their own while others became associated with a particular individual's teaching to which they did not in fact adhere. Arius was probably not "an Arian" in later senses, and Pelagius may not have been Pelagian. Not all those condemned as Arians held to the teachings attributed to him.

18. Montanism was a movement that coalesced in Phrygia ca. 160 CE around a prophet, Montanus, and two prophetesses, Maximilla and Prisca.

19. New teachings included, for example, that the world would end at the death of one of their prophetesses.

20. Some have argued that another significant result of these experiences was their contribution to the long shadow of doubt over the place of women in Church leadership, despite the positive light and roles of leadership in which several women disciples are presented in the New Testament, because of the high profiles that the prophetesses Maximilla and Prisca had within this troublesome group.

21. Named for Marcion, who died ca. 160 CE.

22. Arianism is associated with Arius, c. 260–336 CE, who was denounced and locally excommunicated for his views on Christ and eventually condemned more widely in 325 CE. Here in particular one must be wary of identifying the figure with the wide group of people who were ultimately condemned under his title. See especially Rowan Williams, *Arius: Heresy & Tradition*, rev. ed. (Grand Rapids, MI: Eerdmans, 2002). This heresy is therefore particularly interesting for the Building Bridges Seminar, since from certain "orthodox" points of view Muslims can perhaps be held to have, as it were, at best an Arian view of Christ, in that the Qur'ān is understood explicitly to reject Christ's full divinity.

23. It is important to note, however, that the disagreement was at times as much about the use of the term *ousios* (substance) in this context at all as over whether *homoi* (like) or *homo* (the same) would best qualify it.

24. And this particularly in the light of the contrasts between "Eastern, Greek" and "Western, Latin" patterns of thought, alongside residual Hebraic resonances and local Semitic dialects.

25. Perhaps rather, finding common expression of the common mind that the Church in some sense already had in Christ Jesus.

26. The potentially toxic mix of theological convictions with local loyalties is also evidenced in the Church's debate with Donatism (Africa, fourth through seventh centuries, named after Donatus, one of their bishops, who died in exile in 355 CE). Some purists in Carthage refused to allow any priests who had abandoned their faith in times of persecution to return to office, asserting that only pure, holy ministers can truly make the sacrament present. With rival bishops, they set up a separatist church, requiring converts to be rebaptized by their (more holy) ministers. These differences played into feelings of high-handed treatment and were in fact further enflamed by condemnations, excommunications, and exiles. Here again debate was about who had authority over whom as well as about what the Church should be like and how one might be saved. The responses were various, including the apparently petty and political as well as the persistently pastoral and theological, particularly in the work of St. Augustine, Bishop of Hippo, whose own journey of conversion made him acutely aware that the Church, although called to be holy and to be a holy presence in the world, was in fact full of sinners in need of redemption, including her ministers. It was not the holiness—or otherwise—of the human minister that guaranteed—or threatened—the holiness of the sacrament but rather the holiness of Christ himself, the true minister of any sacrament. The apostolicity, the faithfulness of the Church, and the holiness and authority of her ministers did not depend on the holiness of those ministers but precisely only on their shared reliance on Christ's holiness. He also argued that any Christian could baptize: becoming a member of the Church did not require the presence of any other "minister" than a Christian—and (very importantly for future relationships between separate churches) could never be repeated. Here, again, theological and even schismatic debate, essentially about the nature of holiness, the makeup of the one Church, the possibility and nature of any limits to God's salvific grace, and the locations of authority to rule on these matters, was central in honing of orthodox Christian doctrine, increasing ecclesial self-understanding and commitments to unity but thereby excluding others.

27. Alongside these one should also include other ancient Christian communities, such as those in Syria, which grew up into local churches largely in isolation from the greater gatherings of other Christians, with their own sets of texts and idiosyncratic liturgies and theology. There have been many studies in recent years, particularly in the light of twentieth-century ecumenical endeavors and in growing recognition of the ways in which local and

imperial politics were often unhelpfully embroiled in what later generations have tended to read as purely theological debates, attempting rehabilitations of many of the groups, which were once regarded as "schismatic heretics" (and particularly those which persisted as churches). Perhaps they should be regarded as "heterodox" rather than "heretical."

28. To attempt, as in this section, to describe two of the most significant, painful, thoughtful separations of such a complex community in a couple of paragraphs is preposterous in the extreme (not least because I would not have the scholarship or expertise to provide more nuanced detailed accounts even if I were given more time); it also threatens merely to reinforce stereotype and division. I make the attempt primarily in the hope of introducing the novice to these events, the debates surrounding them and their widely perceived lineaments, in the belief that these will assist a greater understanding of the increasing variety of Christian church extant in the world today as well as the modern attempts to "undo" some of our divisions. The Great Schism is also sometimes referred to as the Schism of the East, to distinguish it from the later Schism of the West, 1378 to 1417, in which there were two, and later three, rival popes battling for power. While often referred to as the "Eastern" Orthodox Church, the Orthodox Church is by no means "all of the East"—there have always been other Churches in that geographical area; neither is it to be confined to the ancient "East"— the Church spread north into Europe and (furthermore) there are Eastern Orthodox congregations, from different Orthodox churches, in dispersal throughout most of the world. Helpful accounts of Orthodox history and identity can be found in Timothy (now Kallistos) Ware's *The Orthodox Church: New Edition* (New York: Penguin, 1993) and John Anthony McGuckin's *The Orthodox Church: An Introduction to Its History, Doctrine and Spiritual Culture* (Malden, MA: Wiley Blackwell, 2008).

29. The day when the Spirit descended upon the gathered disciples and blessed them with the gift of tongues to preach the Gospel to the nations; one of the traditional "birthpoints" of the Church.

30. That is, they did not recognize the pope's claim to universal jurisdiction.

31. Nicholas Lossky, "B. The Orthodox Church," in "Orthodoxy" by Jean-Yves Lacoste in his *Encyclopedia of Christian Theology*, Vol. II (Oxford: Routledge, 2004), 1168–69. Lossky is not alone in hoping that a post-medieval Orthodoxy might be able to accommodate a different, more congenial interpretation of the term.

32. The description of "two lungs of the Church" is famously used by Pope John Paul II (for example, in the 1995 encyclical *Ut unum sint*, para. 54). I am grateful to Brandon Gallaher for the information that he is alluding to the Russian poet Vyacheslav Ivanov's explanation of his own conversion from Orthodoxy to Catholicism, which allowed him to breathe "with both lungs." For some helpful comments on this, see Robert Bird, *The Russian Prospero: The Creative Universe of Viacheslav Ivanov* (Madison: University of Wisconsin Press 2006), 40 and 289. Although it originates in a modern context, the phrase seems to apply equally well to the more ancient relationship.

33. Many non–Roman Catholics recognize some primacy for the See of Peter but are not willing to acknowledge either the universal jurisdiction or infallibility claimed by Roman Catholic dogma for the papal office. (Some Roman Catholics are also troubled in conscience by these concepts.)

34. The debates of the Reformation are often seen as prefigured in the work of John Wycliffe to oppose excessive papal power and translate the Bible in England in the later 1300s, and usually dated to events in the life of Martin Luther in Germany 1517–21.

35. Hence the later label of "Protestant" for the churches that did rise up from their struggles. Alister McGrath has published several helpful introductory books to the Protestant debates, including *Reformation Thought: An Introduction*, 4th ed. (Oxford: Wiley-Blackwell, 2012).

36. They included suspicion of papal power and additional burdens that the Church seemed to be placing on believers; the conviction that loyalty to Christ demanded loyalty to scripture rather than to the Church; that human relationships with God were to be mediated by Christ himself and not by priests of the Church; and that mature, faithful Christians should make their own religious decisions based on their own reading of scripture and on teaching heard in their own languages. In particular there were fears that both the cult and the body of dogma had grotesquely outgrown what were required or permitted by scripture, and that paganism and superstition had taken root, if not in the lives of Church leaders, then certainly in the minds and lives of ordinary members of the Church.

37. This echoes much New Testament teaching; see, for example, Paul in Romans 3:27–31: "Then what becomes of our boasting? It is excluded. On what principle? On the principle of works? No, but on the principle of faith. For we hold that a man is justified by faith apart from works of law. Or is God the God of Jews only? Is he not the God of Gentiles also? Yes, of Gentiles also, since God is one; and he will justify the circumcised on the ground of their faith and the uncircumcised through their faith. Do we then overthrow the law by this faith? By no means! On the contrary we uphold the law!" (This would be another interesting passage for consideration of the early and continuing debates in the Church about the place of the law, and the relationships between Jews and Gentiles, in the new Covenant.) But see also the discussion of faith and works in James 2:14–26: "What does it profit, my brethren, if a man says he has faith but has not works? Can his faith save him? . . . Faith, by itself, if it has no works, is dead. . . . Show me your faith apart from your works, and I by my works will show you my faith. . . . 'Abraham believed God, and it was reckoned to him as righteousness.' . . . a man is justified by works and not by faith alone. . . . For as the body apart from the spirit is dead, so faith apart from works is dead."

38. That is, to stop challenging the hierarchy and return to appropriate and humble ecclesial obedience—many were priests who had made specific feudal oaths to their bishops and the pope. Only later, in its Counter-Reformation, did the Roman Catholic Church begin gradually to address the issues that had been raised and embrace the protesters' prophetic reminder that the Church, as an undeniably human institution as well as anything else, is in need of constant self-criticism, repentance, conversion, judgment, and reform.

39. The sacrament of baptism persisted as the means of admission to this community, but the expression of faith became particularly central to the rite; the sacrament of the Eucharist persisted, too, understood not so much as a sacramental liturgy but more as a memorial fellowship, recalling Christ's Last Supper with his friends and his one and only true sacrifice of himself on the cross. Ministers were generally no longer described as priests, and the Eucharist was not seen as a sacrifice, for in his sacrifice, made once for all, Christ was understood to have replaced all other sacrifice (both past and future) and at the same time also to have shown himself to be the one true High Priest who had replaced all other priests (again, both past and future). Only these two "dominical" sacraments, with direct links to Christ's instruction, are usually recognized in most Protestant churches—other churches have more. For the institution of the Eucharist, see Paul's words (recited in some form at every celebration of the Eucharist) in 1 Corinthians 11:23–26: ". . . on the night when he was betrayed, he took bread and when he had given thanks, he broke it and said, 'This is my body which

is given for you. Do this in remembrance of me.' In the same way after supper he took the cup and said, 'This is the cup of the new covenant in my blood. Do this, as often as you drink it, in remembrance of me.'" For the command to baptize, see Jesus's words at the end of Matthew's Gospel, 28:18–20: "And Jesus said to them, 'All authority in heaven and on earth has been given to me. Go therefore make disciples of all nations, baptising them in the name of the Father and of the Son and of the Holy Spirit, teaching them to observe all that I have commanded you; and lo, I am with you always, to the close of the age.'"

40. For example, the United Reformed Church in the United Kingdom, made from the union of the Presbyterian Church of England and the Congregational Church in England and Wales in 1972; or in Germany the Evangelische Kirche Deutschlands formed from the "Reformed" and "Lutheran" churches (based on the teachings of Calvin and Luther, respectively) of different provinces. Anglicanism provides an intriguing example of a Church, or rather a communion, which on the one hand clearly emerges from the Reformation but which (in some parts at least) has understood itself as in significant continuity with the Church from which it sprang: "Reformed and Catholic" for some; just "reformed" or just "catholic" for others. In its holding together of vastly different theologies and understandings of Church within itself, it offers a (sometimes salutary) example for some visions of Church unity.

41. The World Council of Churches grew out of Protestant movements and endeavors, but the Orthodox Church joined in 1961 and the Roman Catholic Church sends representatives. World Council of Churches *Constitution*, article 1. The current *Constitution* can be found at http://www.oikoumene.org/en/resources/documents/assembly/2013-busan/adopted -documents-statements/wcc-constitution-and-rules (accessed September 29, 2014).

42. A significant aspect of this type of development is that it in some sense reflects early Church decisions over the place of circumcision, for the words of condemnation are not always simply rescinded but often come to be (re)read as applicable to a certain place and time and not necessarily extending to apply equally to the historical inheritors of those communities or in new contexts.

43. For example, the emergence of a "baptismal ecclesiology" that understands membership of the Church through baptism, and so recognizes in the members of other churches members of the one true Church.

44. For example, to put it horribly crassly, the Orthodox can remind others of the importance of worship and liturgy as central elements of the Church; the Catholics can remind others of the importance of doctrine and church order; the Protestants can remind others of the importance of mission and social justice.

45. "Theology may be impossible in the situation of a divided church, its proper agent not being extant. [But to] live as the church in the situation of a divided church—if this can happen at all—must at least mean that we confess we live in radical self-contradiction and that by every churchly act we contradict that contradiction." Jenson, *Systematic Theology*, I, vii. This self-contradiction is part of the Church's eschatological character.

Unity and Disunity in the Life of the Muslim Community

FERAS HAMZA

Unity of community for the earliest Muslims must have meant unifying leadership. Even when that unity would come to take on an increasingly outward form, that is when it became a "living tradition" principally through the performance of acts of communal worship; it was only under a unifying political leadership that the defining boundaries of the community could be drawn. Through his leadership—religious in its genesis, but necessarily political given the social-political consequences of the message—the Prophet was able to bring together diverse elements of Meccan, Medinan and, to some extent, wider Arabian society into a fairly cohesive and independent community. The new religio-political community became cohesive in terms of its devotional and ritual praxis, and independent in terms of its socioeconomic bonds.

This fledgling and delicate polity faced its initial crisis with the death of its founder in 632 CE, with the question of the succession to the Prophet:[1] that this was a critical question is indicated by the fact that all religio-political divisions in Islam—indeed, sectarianism itself—have their origins in the debates over the rightful leadership of the community.[2] So much of import was seen to reside in the issue of the rightful leadership that a caliph was assassinated, a minor battle ensued between prominent companions involving members of the Prophet's family, and two major civil wars broke out a little more than two decades after the Prophet's death.[3] The fact that the first truly fragmenting event, the first civil war, would be recorded by the earliest historical narratives as the *fitna*, a term that connotes "religious trial," clearly attests to the fact that at the heart of this political struggle was a fundamental religious question, that is, the unity of the community.

Indeed, we might usefully introduce here some Qurʾānic references that speak to the urgency of remaining a united community. Q. 3:105 says, "And hold fast, all together, to God's cord and do not become divided," reminding the believers a few lines later, in the same verse, that they had been "enemies but then He [God] brought your hearts together so that you became brothers by His grace when you had been on the brink of a pit of Fire whereat He saved you therefrom."[4] Clearly the unity of the community under the Prophet contrasted with memories of tribal divisions and social enmity in pre-Islamic Arabia. But unity also spoke to what ought to have been a unique feature of this newest of the Abrahamic monotheistic communities, and this is also captured in several Qur'ānic verses, one of which says, "And do not be like those who became divided and differed after manifest signs had come to them; for such there will be a great chastisement" (Q. 3:105). Indeed these verses are part of a larger passage that culminates in the oft-repeated self-description of the Muslim community as being "the best community brought forth for mankind, bidding what is decent and forbidding what is wrong and having faith in God." Obviously, in this depiction, division heralded the presence of religious misguidance in the community.

The first civil war proved to be the slippery slope toward sectarianism, the very kind of schism against which the Qur'ān had warned. But well before the first Muslim civil war, in the caliphate of Abu Bakr, the unity of the community was tested. The first caliph's brief two-year reign was almost entirely consumed with the reunification of the Arabian tribes under the authority of the Medinan caliphate. The mass tribal rebellions that took place across Arabia shortly after the Prophet's death could not have been more than political defections in the sense that Medina's right to continue to exercise political (and fiscal) authority over the entire peninsula was being questioned. And although this questioning of Medinan authority was not based on any theological misgivings or reinterpretation of the religious paradigm, these rebellions came to be known as the Wars of Apostasy (ridda), that is, the rejection of Medina's political authority was very much seen an act of sacrilege. Clearly, then, unity of the religious community in the earliest period depended upon the stabilization of the political community, the political community becoming stabilized not only through ritual (which would take a far longer time to stabilize) but through the receipt of religious taxes (zakāt) by the Medinan caliphate; only this way could the political community become financially autonomous and acquire the momentum to invest back in itself. This expansion of Medinan authority is reflected in the expansion of the Muslim community in the period of the conquests.

From 634 to 644 CE, the period of the second caliph, ʿUmar, most of the central lands of what is now the Middle East, including Iran to the east and Egypt to the west, had been successfully incorporated under Medina's authority.

A fledgling religious community had burgeoned into an empire, and most of the growing pains of this new religious endeavor had been temporarily absorbed by these rapid geographical expansions. Soon, however, the dust was settling over a vastly transformed landscape in which other centers of power had emerged to challenge Medina's prerogative to administer the affairs of the larger Muslim community. The first such challenge came from the governor of Damascus, Muʿāwiya ibn ʿAbī Sufyān, who had enjoyed this position since the time of the second caliph, ʿUmar, and retained it throughout the caliphate of his kinsman, ʿUthmān. When the imām ʿAlī assumed the caliphate in 656, his recalling of provincial governors and request for the traditional pledge of allegiance was summarily refused by Muʿāwiya, who justified his stance by claiming that the killers of his kinsman, the previous caliph, ʿUthmān, had not been brought to justice, a duty that he argued was clearly now ʿAlī's. A military standoff would ensue, pitting many of the forces of the Iraqi garrison towns against the Syrian tribesmen backing Muʿāwiya. This standoff came to a head in the Battle of Siffin, which effectively sparked off the first civil war in 657. Most of the Iraqi tribesmen supported Ali on account of what they saw as his legitimate claim to the caliphate/imamate, convinced that it was incumbent on them to bring the recalcitrant Muʿāwiya and his tribesmen into submission. The war cries on both sides railed in religious/Qurʾānic language: for his Iraqi opponents, Muʿāwiya was an imām of misguidance/error (ḍalāl) while Ali was the one of hudā (guidance), and vice versa for the Syrian supporters of Muʿā-wiya.[5] There then followed the infamous event of the arbitration where an apparent call for a truce was made by the Syrians with the offer that an arbiter be chosen from either side in order to negotiate a solution to the crisis.

To make a long story short, this call to arbitration was initially supported by certain pious elements in ʿAlī's camp who probably had in mind the Qurʾānic verse, "And if two groups of the faithful should fight one another, make peace between them. But if one party aggresses against the other, fight the one which aggresses until it returns to God's ordinance. Then if it returns, make peace between them equitably and be just. Indeed God loves the just. The faithful are indeed brothers. Therefore make peace between your brothers and be wary of God, so that you may receive [His] mercy" (49:9–10). However, when suspicions arose, which the caliph ʿAlī himself had entertained, that the Syrians were stalling for time and, as things turned out, were able to subvert the arbitration in their favor, the very same pious elements now vehemently egged ʿAlī on to resume the hostilities against Muʿāwiya and the Syrians. Explaining to them that he could not very well break the terms of the truce until he had good reason to, they issued him a warning that he should "repent" (*tawba*), as they themselves admitted that they had, or else face an insurrection.

Negotiations between ʿAlī and the same elements who had now seceded to a different location culminated in the assassination of ʿAlī's messenger. The first schism in Islam had been borne. The group of secessionists came to be known as the Khawārij (Kharijites). The historical sources record their position as having been based on the idea that when an imām proves himself to be in error and does not repent and mend his ways, it is legitimate—indeed, obligatory—to oppose and replace him with any other Muslim of recognized moral uprightness.

Effectively, what the Kharijite schism brought to the fore was the question of the status of a Muslim once he had committed a serious religious offence, for they could only justify their willingness to oppose ʿAlī (whom they had so vigorously championed originally) by categorically declaring him—and now all those who continued to support him—as unbelievers (*kuffar*). In this instance what may otherwise have been interpreted as a political miscalculation—that is, ʿAlī's prevarication in the case of Muʿāwiya—translated itself into a religious offence: political sins in this context were religious ones.

What the Kharijite position suggested was that there was no theological category for Muslim grave sinners, at least no way to accommodate them within the political community: all relations were off and such a sinner's blood and property became licit in the view of these early schismatics. ʿAlī was now faced with another battle front on his own side. Before he could turn to deal with Muʿāwiya, he had to deal with the rebels first—since, not only were they a danger to the campaign against the Syrians, they were also wreaking havoc in and around the major garrison town of Kufa, ʿAlī's mainstay of tribal support. The caliph eventually engaged them further up the Tigris at a site called al-Nahrawan in the year 658, eliminating a large number of these rebels, but clearly not all of them. Three years later, one such Kharijite sympathizer struck the caliph in revenge as he prayed in the central mosque in Kufa. The caliph did not recover from his wound.

Although a minority within the larger Muslim body, the Kharijites' stance ended up producing more theology in this period than they could have imagined. Thus was born the question of the status of the Muslim grave sinner, or as he would later be redefined, the sinning believer.[6] Debates about the unity of the community continued to center on the issue of righteous leadership, but it was becoming increasingly clear that this one office could not accommodate the sundry and rival claims being made to fill it. If unity could not be achieved under political leadership, then it had to be achieved in other ways. If the political reality did not seem to reflect a broad religious unity—that is to say, if the political community with its emerging divisions could no longer be understood theologically—then theology had to be rethought to accommodate the political reality.

We move now chronologically to a parallel development, one that was beginning to manifest clearly among those who continued to champion ʿAlī's imamate after the Kharijite schism. I say parallel because although it must have been somewhat instigated by the Kharijite defection, it was not concerned so much with the theological consequences of political misdeeds as it was with the status of the leadership that it championed. The Kharijites, though depicted as zealots and fanatics, were mostly an extremely pious element, and many morally well-regarded individuals were among their ranks. Their slaughter could not have sat very comfortably with the wider community, and yet clearly an individual of the religious uprightness of the imām ʿAlī could not be reproached for seeking to quell the strife in the community. Those who had remained loyal to him must have been forced to consider at length the merits of his leadership and perhaps justify for themselves, now more than ever, their ongoing belief in his superior merits.

Though it is clear that the imām ʿAlī enjoyed considerable support in the Iraqi camps, in Kufa in particular, the sort of theological arguments justifying his period of rule do not emerge during his lifetime. But they do soon thereafter. After ʿAlī's assassination, Muʿāwiya was able to consolidate his power and secure the title of caliph. However, memories of this usurpation had not faded in the Iraqi camps, and the question of the rightful leadership of the community passed onto the following generation. Muʿāwiya's caliphate was inherited by his son Yazīd in 680. The latter's opprobrious behavior quickly became a cause for concern and a context for, once again, staking rival claims to the caliphate.

Al-Ḥusayn, the second son of ʿAlī, had assumed his father's mantle and received support from the very same Iraqi camps that had supported his father. With promises of broad support and a guarantee of a sizeable turnout, the Kufans had written to al-Ḥusayn in Medina to join them and stake his rightful claim to the caliphate by challenging Muʿāwiya's son, the caliph Yazīd. This proved to be an abortive venture as the support never fully materialized. Al-Ḥusayn and a small band of followers, including family members, were intercepted by Yazīd's forces and massacred at the famous Battle of Karbalāʾ on the tenth day of Muḥarram, in 680 CE.

Much more than his father's death, al-Ḥusayn's death was seen as an act of martyrdom for the sake of a just cause in the face of tyranny. This event would be seminal for the emerging Shīʿa and for forging a distinct religious identity in Islam—one that would henceforth nourish itself intellectually and devotionally on the assertion that the Prophet's family—precisely ʿAlī and his descendants—enjoyed a superior religious status, recognition of which entailed true belief and, ultimately, secured salvation in the Hereafter. This was an exclusivist claim in two senses: it narrowed down and highlighted a particular kind of religious leadership, and it could not accommodate the increasing diversity of Muslim religio-political loyalties. Unity, with its implicit theological and eschatological import, from the emerging Shīʿi perspective would henceforth lay circumscribed and isolated among that community that recognized the salvific element of devotional loyalty (*walaya*) to a line of descendants of the Prophet, that which we might call the "imamic truth / reality"; that unity could no longer be shared with everyone else who subscribed to the Muslim community, whether nominally or simply through the shared exterior praxis of the faith. Shīʿism had constructed its own "charismatic" community within the larger Muslim community.[7]

Between these two polar opposites, the Kharijite schism and the emerging Shīʿi identity, lay quite a vast silent majority who had not thus far expressed themselves explicitly on religio-political matters but who were now viewing the nonuniversalism of both stances with increasing concern. Shortly after the martyrdom event of al-Ḥusayn, political turmoil and other challenges to the Damascus caliphate of the Umayyads, now from the Ḥijāz, resulted in a second major civil war. This second *fitna* drew largely upon the fault lines established in the first war: what remained of the Kharijite movement splintered into three or four other subgroups, and the Shīʿi movement—though far from theologically mature—acquired more momentum.

However, a major difference now was the emergence of an antisectarian stance in this period, the very expression of the silent majority alluded to earlier, in the form of a position called *irjaʾ*, or the "suspension of judgment." Those who upheld this view, Murjiʾites (from the same verbal root, *irjaʾ*), argued that all dispute about the merits or demerits of the early caliphs (they meant ʿUth-mān and ʿAlī) had to cease: they argued this precisely to stem the rising tide of sectarianism by undermining its very religio-political premises. These Murjiʾites were certainly a significant group because they were in effect representing a considerable constituency within the wider community who had not hitherto justified their religio-political leanings but who were, so to speak, happy to go along with the government of the day. They were articulating for the first time what would become essential Sunnī theology—namely, that profession of the faith (islām) was enough to ensure membership of the political community. In fact, they came up with the label of muʾmin dall (misguided believer), which—however oxymoronic it may seem—allowed for a huge gray category that embraced all political leanings and did not require an overintrusive inspection of one's religious comportment.

To Khārijites and Shīʾites, the category made no sense. However, to the large majority and to a particular emerging group of scholars, the "traditionists" (ahl al-ḥadīth), it only lacked a slight adjustment: its eschatological import had to be accounted for.[8] What would happen to these sinning or misguided believers in the Hereafter? For many of these traditionists, coexistence with such a cate-gory could not be justified without a concomitant adjustment in the salvation theology. There was one other pragmatic matter that could not be overlooked. Upright religious behavior should always be sought and encouraged, and a dilu-tion of this rigor by explicitly extending the status of Muslim/believer to all who simply professed the faith threatened to set a bad moral example; it certainly placed no emphasis on "works" (ʿamal) that were considered inseparable from the ontology of a believer.

Sunnī theology, as it coalesced by the middle of the third century AH (ninth century CE), would now allow for the communal solidarity it envisioned by making it explicit in its classical creeds that all those who professed the faith would eventually be saved—sinning believers included—though they might have to undergo a temporary punishment in Hellfire beforehand.[9]

But why did the proto-Sunnīs—whether Murjiʾites or traditionists—want to keep the community together when most of it could not care less or had con-sciously opted out?[10] Here we might go back and consider what was mentioned earlier of both the nature of the community under the Prophet as a united and thereby distinct community and the various Qurʾānic reminders that division had been the perennial bane of religious communities in the past. What made this community "the best community brought forth for mankind" was the

Prophet himself, the last and the most excellent of the messengers. If only the community could be kept together in the here and now, however loosely or compromisingly, they would be together as the people of Paradise in the Hereafter. This was essentially proclaimed in possibly the earliest Islamic monument we have, the Dome of the Rock. Constructed by the caliph ʿAbd al-Malik b. Marwān, the victor of the second civil war, it was completed in what came to be known as the Year of Unity (ʿam al-jamāʿa) in 691–92. That unity was articulated in one of the inner mosaic inscriptions in which the following supplication is made: "Muhammad is the Messenger of God, may God bless him and accept his intercession on behalf of his community on the Day of Resurrection."[11]

Clearly, if Sunnism was to remain committed to the idea of communal unity or solidarity (Sunnī were, after all, known as the ahl al-sunna wa'l-jamāʿa), it had to rethink the nature of the political office and religious leadership. Unlike the Kharijites and the Shiites, the Sunnī achieved this by redefining the nature of political leadership at least in terms of its significance for the ultimate salvation of the community. With the rise to prominence in this period of the hadīth scholars, the traditionists, Prophetic authority was no longer seen to reside in the office of the imamate but in the texts that recorded the Prophetic model behavior, the sunna. Salvation was no longer dependent upon righteous leadership. (It could not be, as the caliphate had been usurped—first by the Umayyads, then the Abbasids.) Rather, it could be found individually in the mass of circulating hadīth texts by all those who chose to emulate the Prophet through his guidance and his paradigmatic behavior: that was the argument of the Sunni scholars.

The caliphs resisted for a while, insisting that their political leadership was also religious, that they had a principal role in religious affairs—in praxis, law, and theology.[12] The standoff between the scholars and the caliphs came to a head during the caliphate of the famous al-Maʾmūn, who instigated a mihna (religious inquisition) in 833 CE to challenge the right of the hadīth scholars to be guardians of religious knowledge and to stake a claim for religious authority. This inquisition was a failure, as the Sunnī scholars stood their ground and found support among the wider public who accorded them the status of religious leaders.

After the abolition of the mihna fifteen years later in 848, it was clear that—for the large majority of Muslims—the interpreters of the law would not be any one individual but an undefined body of scholars whose claim to authority was simply that they had dedicated themselves to studying the Qurʾān and the texts of the Prophetic sunna. Political office was not dispensable, however, for it was still important for many other practical functions (the defense of the borders, the guardianship of the annual ḥajj, security, and fiscal affairs). Sunnism did not envision a separation of "church and state"—that is, between religious affairs and nonreligious ones—but a division of labor in which both political leadership and, now, the religious leadership of the scholars would ensure a healthy religious society.

The Abbasid patronage of Sunnism from after the abolition of the *miḥna* meant a recognition of the diffuse nature of religious authority in the Sunni perspective—diffuse in the sense that it was no longer concentrated in any one lineage, individual, or caliph—and could in fact be attained by anyone who committed themselves to a scholastic career.[13] This diffusion of authority would be a hallmark of Sunnism and would allow it to absorb all manner of political government, including that of the slave soldiers as well as Shīʿi dynasties—including Fāṭimid Ismāʿīlis in Egypt, North Africa, and the Levant (909–1171), and the Zaydi-Twelver Buyids in Iraq and Iran (945–1055) during a period known to historians as the Shīʿi century where the majority of the populations remained Sunnī. To this absorption may be added the Turkic Seljuks (1055–1194), the Mongols (thirteenth century), the Mamluks (1250–1517), and eventually the Ottomans (thirteenth century–1922).

Shīʿism, too, has had to make its own compromise with the political state; for most of its history it has had to figure out what to do in the absence of the historical imāms (an absence effective from about ca. 900), who were considered by their followers the only legitimate interpreters of the Qurʾān and the Prophetic sunna, and hence the very Law (sharīʿa) itself. The story of Shīʿism, like Sunnism, is also the story of the rise of the ʿulamāʾ. And although this is not immediately obvious, just as the Sunni ʿulamāʾ were content to leave politics and government to various dynasties (caliphs and sultans), so too the Shīʿi ʿulamāʾ decided that by giving political legitimacy to dynasties (historically, the most important of which were the Safavids, ca. 1500–1700), they could secure their own guardianship, spiritual and legal, of the community (in the absence of the imāms). From about the time of the major occultation of the twelfth imām (ca. 941) to the emergence of the Shīʿi Safavid state in Iran (1501–1722), Shīʿi communities, in the main, had run their own affairs, relying on leading scholars for the interpretation of the key texts as well as the administration of the alms taxes (*zakāt*). From the seventeenth century, with the rise of the Uṣūlī school of Twelver Shīʿism and its eventual victory over another major tradition in Twelver Shīʿism, that of the *akhbarī* school, the power, authority, and independent juristic capacity of the Shiʾi *ʿulamāʾ* are definitively enhanced.[14]

Akhbarī Twelver Shīʿism seemed to have much in common with the Sunnī schools in the sense that they gave priority to the key texts, in this case the Qurʾān and the Prophetic sunna in the form of reports (*akhbar*) transmitted from the historical imāms. But the real point behind the Akhbari position was a rejection of the Uṣūlī school's fairly broad acceptance of *ijtihād* (independent jurisprudential reasoning)—which, if accepted, ultimately allowed for an unbridled expansion of the Shīʿi scholar's (*ʿalim*) remit, effectively displacing that of the historical imām. With the rise of the Shīʿi Safavids in 1500, the Safavid state looked to the Shīʿi *ʿulamāʾ* in order to consolidate its legitimacy, particularly in the face of the growing Sunni Ottoman Empire. This was an opportunity for the Shīʿi *ʿulamāʾ* to consolidate their own authority vis-à-vis their Shīʿi communities, especially once the Safavid state collapsed, when the Shīʿi *ʿulamāʾ* momentarily found themselves without effective state patronage. It is at this point during the early part of the eighteenth century that the Uṣūlī school came to dominate, almost entirely displacing the Akhbarī school.[15]

Notwithstanding twentieth-century *taqrīb* ("bringing closer together") initiatives to bridge the divide between Sunnī and Shīʿi, sectarianism had been ingrained so early on in Islamic history that it could never really transcend its divisions into a pan-Islamic ecumenical project. Sunnī Ottoman and Shīʿi Safavid political and geographical rivalry only affirmed the divisions between Sunnism and Shīʿism. Even when Muslim revivalist and reformist movements emerged (arguably from the time of Ibn Taymiyya under the Mongols through the Indian reform movements of the sixteenth to seventeenth centuries[16]), they did so within the contexts of the broader sectarian divide, at least in the sense that reformism did not seek to eradicate the sectarian divide (in the case of the Wahhābī reform movement, it actually reiterated it).[17]

Pan-Islamic movements of the late nineteenth and early twentieth century were momentarily ecumenical, if at all. And when the Islamic world was redrawn geographically, politically, and culturally along the lines of the modern nation-state during the last century, the medieval religious divisions persisted, now in more localized form. *Umma*, as a paracolonial term, has certainly become more prominent in Muslim discourse in the twentieth and twenty-first centuries, and as a concept of the imaginary, undoubtedly intended as a socially binding concept existing in a somewhat tense, or at least undefined, relationship to nationalism.[18] Like nationalism, *umma* is at once vague yet potentially dynamic and just as animating. A recent contribution on the idea of "community" in Islam—in answering the author's own rhetorical question, "Does a global Muslim community exist? Has it ever existed?"—asserts a categorical "no."[19]

The author's argument is that "such an objectified community does not exist, and . . . has never existed on any socially significant scale." Such a denial of communal awareness is intended by the author as a corollary to the idea that "religious community is more often imagined than real, prescribed than actualized." But I would contend that an appreciation of the multiplicity of visions within Islam of Islam does not require a denial of this "imagined community." Is an imagined community any less real than a physical/political one? I do not think so at all; and Ṣūfīs, about whom nothing has been said in this essay, certainly could transcend the sectarian divide, and, moreover, they themselves articulated an imaginary experience (namely, the spiritual path) as nothing but ultimate reality. Indeed, denying the power of the imaginary hardly does justice to the religious experience itself. And although I have devoted the bulk of this essay to the historical record as it reveals the history of disunity, there is much to be said that is perhaps not in the historical record, but that is just as "true" or "real," emotive and binding, and hence "communal," in the devotional language, common praxis, and sacred referents of each individual Muslim.[20]

Notes

1. For a detailed treatment of the events of the period, see W. Madelung, *The Succession to Muhammad: A Study of the Early Caliphate* (Cambridge: Cambridge University Press, 1997).

2. The best introduction to the early sectarian movements as well as questions of legitimate leadership, faith, and works remains W. Montgomery Watt's *The Formative Period of Islamic Thought* (Edinburgh: Edinburgh University Press, 1973).

3. The third caliph, ʿUthmān b. ʿAffān, was assassinated in his home in Medina by malcontents who had initially come to voice their discontent with him in person but whose grievances ended up falling on deaf ears. The fact that they were able to intimidate the caliph and later return to murder him without much interference from others suggests a certain degree of sympathy for the rebels and a wider dissatisfaction with his caliphate. The confrontation was known as the Battle of the Camel because the Prophet's wife, ʿĀʾisha, famously rode out into battle on a camel, supported by two prominent companions—Ṭalḥa and Zubayr, of notable Meccan origins—against the Prophet's own cousin and son-in-law ʿAlī b. ʿAbī Ṭālib. The battle broke out fairly soon after ʿAlī had assumed the caliphate in 656 (following Uthmān's assassination) and was successfully dealt with by him. The two companions were killed in the skirmishes, and the Prophet's wife returned to Medina after a personal

reprimand from the caliph. The first civil war was known as the *Fitna* (657–61) and the second civil war took place during 685–91.

4. All Qur'ānic translations are from ʿAlī Qulī Qaraʾi, *The Qur'an with a Phrase-by-Phrase English Translation* (London: ICAS Press, 2004).

5. Iraq and Syria in this period (late seventh century) may be considered as two quite distinct administrative provinces that were indirectly controlled by the caliphate in Medina. Iraq consisted principally of the garrison town of Kufa (modern-day Najaf) and to the south, Basra. The Syrian province centered around Damascus and can be thought of as coextensive with Roman Syria Magna. The mostly Arabian tribesmen who would populate these centers with the conquests ended up supporting rival candidates from the Prophet's tribe, the Quraysh, for the caliphate.

6. The only really detailed discussion of the question of the sinning Muslim believer remains that of P. Crone and F. Zimmermann, *The Epistle of Salim Ibn Dhakwan* (Oxford: Oxford University Press, 2001), esp. 186–250. A more contextual outline can be gleaned from M. A. Cook's *Early Muslim Dogma: A Source-Critical Study* (Cambridge: Cambridge University Press, 1981). (See his comments to the nonspecialist reader, viii–ix.) The authoritative work of J. van Ess remains standard reading on Muslim theology of the early period; see J. van Ess, "The Beginnings of Islamic Theology," in *The Cultural Context of Medieval Learning*, ed. J. E. Murdoch and E. D. Sylla, 87–112 (Boston: D. Reidel, 1975); J. van Ess, *The Flowering of Muslim Theology*, trans. Jane Marie Todd (Cambridge, MA: Harvard University Press, 2006); and his masterwork, J. van Ess, *Theologie und Gesellschaft im 2. und 3. Jahrhundert Hidschra*, 6 vol. (Berlin: Walter de Gruyter, 1991–95).

7. On this aspect of the Shīʿi identity within the broader Muslim community, see the excellent monograph by Maria Massi Dakake, *The Charismatic Community: Shi'ite Identity in Early Islam* (Albany: State University of New York Press, 2007).

8. On the development of ḥadīth in early Islam, see I. Goldziher, *Muslim Studies* (Muhammedanische Studien), vol. 2, ed. S. M. Stern, trans. C. R. Barber and S. M. Stern (London: George Allen and Unwin, 1971).

9. See F. Hamza, "Temporary Hell-Fire Punishment and the Making of Sunni Orthodoxy," in *Roads to Paradise: Eschatology and Concepts of the Hereafter in Islam*, ed. T. Lawson and S. Günther (Leiden: Brill, 2013).

10. I use the term "proto-Sunnīs" here to refer to religio-political expressions that prefigured the crystallization of formal Sunnism in the tenth to eleventh centuries as an umbrella term for four legal schools: Hanafism, Malikism, Shāfiʿism and Hanbalism—which constituted communities of scholars who traced their jurisprudential methods to one of the four eponyms of these schools (Abū Ḥanifa, d. 767; Malik b. Anas, d. 795; Shāfiʿi, d. 820; and Aḥmad ibn Ḥanbal, d. 855).

11. C. Kessler's reproduction, "ʿAbd al-Malik's Inscription in the Dome of the Rock: A Reconsideration," *JRAS* 1 (1970): 2–14; *Répertoire chronologique d'epigraphie arabe*, Institut Français d'Archéologie Orientale du Caire, ed. E. Combe et al. (1931–91), vol. 1, no. 9; and in a photo still in O. Grabar and S. Nuseibeh, *The Dome of the Rock* (New York: Rizzoli, 1996), 98 (upper left corner of page). Incidentally, the concept of the Prophet's eschatological intercession would also be used to bolster the notion that all Muslim grave sinners would ultimately be saved and admitted into Paradise: again, this reflected the political reality of communal disunity and the Sunni attempt to be "catholic" by encompassing all subdivisions.

12. The argument that the caliphs in early Islam enjoyed a religio-political role that was necessary for the salvation of the community was made by P. Crone and M. Hinds in their

God's Caliph: Religious Authority in the First Centuries of Islam (Cambridge: Cambridge University Press, 1986).

13. On Abbasid patronage of Sunnism, see Muhammad Qasim Zaman, *Religion and Politics under the Early Abbasids: The Emergence of the Proto-Sunni Elite* (Leiden: Brill, 1997).

14. For a recent summary of this debate, see Robert M. Gleave, "The Akhbariyya and the Usuliyya," in *Encyclopedia of Islam*, ed. K. Fleet et al., 3rd ed. (Leiden: Brill, 2007).

15. One, of course, could argue—as many are wont to—that with its insistence on the jurisprudential authority and autonomy (*ijtihād*) of the Shīʿi ʿalim, the Uṣūlī school ultimately paved the way for the Shīʿi clerical takeover of the state (namely, Khumayni's Islamic revolution in Iran, post 1979). However, Khumayni's *vilayat al-faqih* (authoritative guardianship of the jurisprudent) could also be seen as an aberrance, even within the Uṣūlī tradition, since for many leading intellectuals (cf. Allama Tabataba'i, d. 1981) no Shīʿi ʿalim could ever replace (or displace) the spiritual guardianship/authority of the historical imāms.

16. On this period of reformism, see Fazlur Rahman, *Revival and Reform in Islam: A Study of Islamic Fundamentalism*, ed. Ibrahim Moosa (Oxford: Oneworld Publications, 2000); and Fazlur Rahman, *Islam*, 2nd ed. (Chicago: Chicago University Press, 1979), esp. 193–234.

17. On the role of the ʿulemāʾ in more recent times and questions of sectarianism, see Muhammad Qasim Zaman, *The Ulamā in Contemporary Islam: Custodians of Change* (Princeton, NJ: Princeton University Press, 2002).

18. Cf. Benedict Anderson, *Imagined Communities: Reflections on the Origin and Spread of Nationalism* (London: Verso, 1983).

19. See Ahmet T. Karamustafa, "Community," in *Key Themes for the Study of Islam*, ed. Jamal J. Elias, 93–103 (Oxford: Oneworld Publications, 2010); contrast with the rich picture portrayed by G. P. Makris, *Islam in the Middle East: A Living Tradition* (Oxford: Blackwell Publishing, 2007).

20. Although, of course, the civilizational heritage of Islam speaks for itself in terms of a shared religious vision, both aesthetic and intellectual.

Scripture Dialogue V
Unity and Disunity in the Church

John 17:20–24

Commentary

These verses come from the "High Priestly Prayer" of Jesus, immediately before his betrayal and crucifixion. Much of the prayer is intercession for the disciples and those who will believe in Jesus through their testimony. As in the passage from Ephesians in chapter 5, so also here the community of the believers is linked to the unity of God. What is more explicit here is the relational nature of the unity of God, which is the source and the model of the unity of the believers. "We are one," says Jesus, the Son, to the Father (v. 22); verse 23 speaks of a mutual indwelling of the Father and the Son, and according to verse 24 this loving unity existed before "the foundation of the world" (cf. the opening of the same gospel, John 1:1–5). Jesus prays to the Father that those who believe in him may "be in us," sharing in the loving unity of the Father and the Son and so living out that unity among themselves.

Biblical text:

[20]"I ask not only on behalf of these [the disciples], but also on behalf of those who will believe in me through their word, [21]that they may all be one. As you, Father, are in me and I am in you, may they also be in us, so that the world may believe that you have sent me. [22]The glory that you have given me I have given them, so that they may be one, as we are one, [23]I in them and you in me, that they may become completely one, so that the world may know that you have sent me and have loved them even as you have loved me. [24]Father, I desire that those also, whom you have given me, may be with me where I am, to see my glory, which you have given me because you loved me before the foundation of the world."

1 Corinthians 1:10–17

Commentary

If in John 17 we have the ideal, the vision of Church unity as it should be, here we have a frank account from Paul of the actual reality of disunity among the Christians in Corinth, who are quarrelling and dividing into factions focused on different Christian teachers. (On Apollos, see Acts 18:24–28; "Cephas" refers to Peter.) There are many other indications in the New Testament of Christian disunity, whether actual or potential, and frequent calls for the need for vigilance in maintaining peace and, where necessary, seeking reconciliation. Paul's brief response at this point is to emphasize the indivisibility of Christ (v. 13) and to refocus attention on the cross of Christ, the heart of Paul's proclamation. Elsewhere, when warning against the divisive influence of selfish ambition, Paul again focuses on the cross, calling believers to seek the same attitude of humility displayed by Jesus (Phil. 2:1–11).

Biblical text:

[10]Now I appeal to you, brothers and sisters, by the name of our Lord Jesus Christ, that all of you should be in agreement and that there should be no divisions among you, but that you should be united in the same mind and the same purpose. [11]For it has been reported to me by Chloe's people that there are quarrels among you, my brothers and sisters. [12]What I mean is that each of you says, "I belong to Paul," or "I belong to Apollos," or "I belong to Cephas," or "I belong to Christ." [13]Has Christ been divided? Was Paul crucified for you? Or were you baptized in the name of Paul? [14]I thank God that I baptized none of you except Crispus and Gaius, [15]so that no one can say that you were baptized in my name. [16](I did baptize also the household of Stephanas; beyond that, I do not know whether I baptized anyone else.) [17]For Christ did not send me to baptize but to proclaim the gospel, and not with eloquent wisdom, so that the cross of Christ might not be emptied of its power.

Scripture Dialogue VI

Unity and Disunity in the Umma

Qur'ān 3:102–5

Commentary

This is another short passage from a section of a Medinan sūra (already cited twice in this selection of texts) particularly concerned with the life of the *umma*. By God's grace, the believers have not only come to a true faith in God, saving them from the fire of punishment in the Hereafter, but have also been reconciled to each other, having previously been in a state of enmity. Such unity, however, is vulnerable and can be easily lost. The believers are to make every effort to hold fast together to the cable (elsewhere translated "rope" or "bond") of God. Note the close parallel in verse 104 to the language of verse 110 (see Scripture Dialogue IV).

Qur'ānic text:

[102]O ye who believe! Observe your duty to God with right observance, and die not save as those who have surrendered (unto Him)

[103]And hold fast, all of you together, to the cable of God, and do not separate. And remember God's favour unto you: How ye were enemies and He made friendship between your hearts so that ye became as brothers by His grace; and (how) ye were upon the brink of an abyss of fire, and He did save you from it. Thus God maketh clear His revelations unto you, that haply ye may be guided,

[104]And there may spring from you a nation who invite to goodness, and enjoin right conduct and forbid indecency. Such are they who are successful.

[105]And be ye not as those who separated and disputed after the clear proofs had come unto them. For such there is an awful doom.

Qur'ān 4:59

Commentary

This is another Medinan passage. The existence of disputes among the believers is acknowledged; where these occur, believers are to refer the matter to God and the messenger. More fully, the first part of the verse instructs believers to obey God, the messenger, "and those of you who are in authority," a text that became of great significance in Islamic political thought.

Qur'ānic text:

O ye who believe! Obey God, and obey the messenger and those of you who are in authority; and if ye have a dispute concerning any matter, refer it to God and the messenger if ye are (in truth) believers in God and the Last Day. That is better and more seemly in the end.

Qur'ān 23:52–53

Commentary

This Meccan passage contrasts the divisions characterizing the religious life of humankind generally with the oneness of Islam and so also, by implication, of the Muslim community.

Qur'ānic text:

[52]And lo! this your religion is one religion and I am your Lord, so keep your duty unto Me.

[53]But they (mankind) have broken their religion among them into sects, each group rejoicing in its tenets.

Qur'ān 49:9–13

Commentary

This is another Medinan passage that acknowledges various ways in which the unity of the *umma* can be endangered. The positive ideal is that the believers should live together as brothers, avoiding abusive language, mutual suspicion, backbiting, and so forth. The much-cited verse 13 widens the frame of reference from believers to "mankind": God has created humans diverse that they "may know one another."

Qur'ānic Text:

[9]And if two parties of believers fall to fighting, then make peace between them. And if one party of them doeth wrong to the other, fight ye that which doeth wrong till it return unto the ordinance of God; then, if it return, make peace between them justly, and act equitably. Lo! God loveth the equitable.

[10]The believers are naught else than brothers. Therefore make peace between your brethren and observe your duty to God that haply ye may obtain mercy.

[11]O ye who believe! Let not a folk deride a folk who may be better than they (are), not let women (deride) women who may be better than they are; neither defame one another, nor insult one another by nicknames. Bad is the name of lewdness after faith. And whoso turneth not in repentance, such are evil-doers.

[12]O ye who believe! Shun much suspicion; for lo! some suspicion is a crime. And spy not, neither backbite one another. Would one of you love to eat the flesh of his dead brother? Ye abhor that (so abhor the other)! And keep your duty (to God). Lo! God is Relenting, Merciful.

[13]O humankind! Lo! We have created you male and female, and have made you nations and tribes that ye may know one another. Lo! the noblest of you, in the sight of God, is the best in conduct. Lo! God is Knower, Aware.

Ḥadīths: The Preference for Unity

Commentary

The following two ḥadīths both state that the main body of the *umma* will stay on the right path, avoiding error and ultimately entering Paradise. The sects that will proliferate are to be avoided; the truth lies with the majority.

Ḥadīth Text: the 73 sects

'Awf ibn Malik reported that the Prophet (Peace be upon him) said: "The Jews split into seventy-one sets: one will enter Paradise and seventy will enter Hell.

The Christians split into seventy-two sects: seventy-one will enter Hell and one will enter Paradise. By Him in Whose hand is my soul, my *Ummah* will split into seventy-two sects: one will enter Paradise and seventy- two will enter Hell." Someone asked, "O Messenger of God, who will they be?" He replied, "The main body of the Muslims (*al- jamāʿa*)."

Commentary

In another version of this ḥadīth the Prophet proceeds to define the saved sect as being "those who follow the Path established by me and my Companions" (Tirmidhī, vol. 2, p. 89).

Ḥadīth Text: The *Umma* Will Not Agree upon Error

"My Community shall never agree upon error, therefore, if you see divergences, you should follow the majority." (Ibn Majah 2:1303 #3950)

Ḥadīth: Muslims as One Brotherhood (from the Farewell Sermon)

Commentary

This passage is not found in all versions of the Farewell Sermon, but it was sufficiently circulated to allow us to refer to it as a normative expression of the early Muslims' understanding and definition of themselves as a community.

Ḥadīth Text: Muslims as One Brotherhood

All mankind is from Adam and Eve. An Arab has no superiority over a non-Arab nor does a non-Arab have any superiority over an Arab; a white person has no superiority over a black person, nor does a black person have any superiority over a white person—except through piety and virtue. Learn that every Muslim is a brother to every Muslim and that the Muslims constitute a single brotherhood. (From the Farewell Sermon)

PART III

Continuity and Change in the Life of the Community

Continuity and Change in the Life of the Community
Muslims' Changing Attitudes to Change

AHMET ALIBAŠIĆ

Today many people in the world keep asking whether Islam and Muslims are capable of change. Is Islam's inability to change the main source of Muslims' frustration? What this question presupposes is that both Islam and Muslims are impervious to change. However, the statement that the only constant in history is change is true for the Muslim community as much as it is for others—even when Muslims themselves would like to believe that they are not changing.

Yet the question is not completely unjustified, as Islamic sources and heritage appear to be ambiguous toward change. On the one hand, Islam is conceived as a complete religion that needs no further refinement. The Qur'ānic verse referring to this completeness, 5:3 (*al-yawm akmaltu lakum dīnakum*), is one of the last Qur'ānic revelations. In addition, the Prophet Muhammad (p.b.u.h.) testified that the first Muslim generations are the best human beings ever to walk this earth (*Ṣaḥīḥ al-Bukhārī*). From these and similar texts, some have understood that any change must mean deterioration and deformation and therefore must be condemned as innovation (*bidʿa*). Things cannot get better. Eventually, according to a ḥadīth, Doomsday will befall the worst of all human beings. Therefore, a regressive view of history (*fasād al-zamān*) was developed. After the best of all times, what else could one expect?

What is more, contextually speaking, Muslims of the first Islamic centuries were in many respects leaders of civilization and felt little outside urge to change what they considered to be a winning formula. Instead, they wanted to preserve and perpetuate it. The very popular Qur'ānic statement (13:11) that "Verily never will God change the condition of a people until they change it themselves (with their own souls)" (*Inna Allāha lā yughayyir mā bi qawmin ḥattā yughayyirū mā bi anfusihim*[1]) was understood in conjunction with another verse (8:53) that implies that the change would be for worse: "Because God will never

87

change the grace which He hath bestowed on a people until they change what is in their (own) souls" (*dhālika bi anna Allāha lam yaku mughayyiran niʿmatan anʿamahā ʿalā qawmin ḥattā yughayyirū mā bi anfusihim*[2]).

For a variety of sociopolitical and practical reasons *taqlīd* (following earlier authorities and generations) became the logical and reasonable way to go.[3] At one point it became dangerous to be innovative, to think. Biographers noted that a scholar so-and-so was "accused of *ijtihād*." Instead of being the highest state a scholar can attain, *ijtihād* became a de facto forbidden exercise. This is one position.

On the other hand, Islam can be and has been understood as a revolutionary message (of egalitarianism, solidarity, etc.) aimed at transforming social realities (*islāḥ*).[4] Furthermore, the message of Islam itself is capable of renewal (*tajdīd*). Independent reasoning (*ijtihād*) is a tool of that renewal. Blameworthy innovation in the ritual matters (*bidʿa, sunnah sayyiʿah*) is to be clearly distinguished from praiseworthy innovation in other areas of human activity (*sunnah ḥasanah*). *Taqlīd* is a way of those who refuse the Message, not its followers: "When it is said to them: 'Follow what God hath revealed:' They say: 'Nay! we shall follow the ways of our fathers.' What! even though their fathers were void of wisdom and guidance?" (2:170).

History is neither regressive nor progressive but cyclical: "Such days (of varying fortunes) We give to men and men by turns" (*tilka ayyām nudāwiluhā bayn al-nās*, 3:140). Change is not necessarily bad news, especially in later centuries, when the condition of the Community became unsatisfying anyway. The emphasis shifted to the Prophetic saying "God will raise, at the head of each century, people for this Community who will renew its religion for it" (*Inna Allāha yabʾathu li hadhihī al-ummah ʿalā raʾs kulli miʾat ʿām man yujaddid lahā dīnahā*). Now grace is in action, movement, and change (*al-barakah fī al-haraka*).

Different Styles of Social Action

This ambiguous or multi-interpretable tradition has resulted, as John Voll notes in his book of twenty years ago, *Islam: Continuity and Change in the Muslim World*, in "different styles of social action," that is, different attitudes toward change among Muslims throughout history, especially in relation to incentives coming from outside the Community either in the context of early Muslim conquests (*futūḥāt*) or colonialism and postcolonialism.[5] One could discern four distinct attitudes to change: accommodation, conservativism, reformism, and militant extremism or fundamentalism.[6]

Accommodation

Many Muslims throughout history have been open to change and willing to adjust to it by pragmatically adapting or simply adopting outside influences in political, intellectual, and even spiritual spheres. Many Muslim rulers from early Umayyads to the nineteenth- and twentieth-century modernizers readily adopted solutions from other political systems. Similarly, certain Muslim intellectuals have done the same in the fields of philosophy, logic, and science in general, starting with ancient Greek and Indian knowledge all the way up to Western scholarship. Perhaps most surprisingly, even spiritual and religious men—most often Sufis, but not them alone—have not resisted the appeal of novel things coming from other traditions or with new times.

On one side, this approach has enabled Muslims to cope with change, connect with others, and build Islamic civilization within a relatively short span of time. Contemporary advocates of this approach have hoped that in our times this will enable Muslims to overcome its many deficiencies and catch up quickly with the developed world. In answer to the question of why this has not happened yet, they point to Muslims' hesitance to adopt Western solutions. In other words, the therapy is correct but has not been taken long enough or in sufficient doses. Of course, accommodation is promoted not only by Westernized Muslims, but they are its most fervent advocates.

While the gains of this approach are undeniable, there have been side effects as well—syncretism, alienation, estrangement, and deviations among them. Those side effects have often provoked reaction in the form of conservativism, reformism, or extreme rejection—which are the other three styles of Muslim response to change.

Conservativism

When compromises and borrowings from other cultures reach visible proportions, they often become disturbing to more conservative segments of the community, who then start emphasizing the need to preserve what was achieved. The fact that there would not have been too much to preserve had it not been for the nonconservative attitude of those who produced those achievements is occasionally missed. The texts and traditions on diminishing sainthood (*wilāyah*) and encouraging mistrust of innovation are given prominence over all others.[7] The *ummah* is reminded that direction is more important than the speed. What is the point of competing on the same track with communities and civilizations whose ultimate goals you may not share? Backwardness is not the worst thing that can happen to the community. Being wrong (*ḍalāl*), following wrong models, and pursuing false aims is the real danger.[8]

This attitude has helped to stabilize the Community and keep the compromises within the generally acceptable range. This in turn has enabled the preservation of gains made by preceding accommodations. Most Muslims of today probably fall within this category.

Yet conservatives are not completely inimical to change. They, too, have invented their own ways and means of dealing with a changing world, mostly predicated on the concepts of necessity and lesser of two evils (*ḍarūra*, *ʿumūm al-balwā*, and *akhaff al-ḍararayn*), or respect for local customs (*ʿurf*, *ʿādah*). Besides, Sunnī traditionalism often verges on accommodationism because of its political conservativism, which considers one hour of political chaos (*fitna*) worse than long periods of tyranny. As Martin van Bruinessen puts it, "Political accommodation is almost a matter of principle in the Sunni tradition, not just one of expedience."[9]

So the early rationalists and later modernists are not the only accommodationists. There is, however, a difference between the two—in the sense that they tend to be active in accommodating changes while traditionalists simply follow what they think they cannot afford not to. This attitude has saved the communities from the misfortunes of social engineering but has exposed them to influence by the negative outside developments much more than by the positive ones. For instance, in political life, this often meant accepting almost every evil that befell or was forced upon the Muslim Community. By insisting on *taqlīd*, most of them have given up the idea of being leaders of change in the first place. Therefore, it should come as no surprise that many traditional Islamic authorities have sided with illiberal modernizers who are against changes such as those promised by the Arab Spring.

Reformism

Where accommodation leads to too many compromises, and where conservativism prevents the community from advancing, reformism sets in. Historically its causes have been syncretism (Ibn Taymiyyah, A. Sirhindi, M. Ibn 'Abd al-Wahhab, Usman dan Fodio), foreign aggression (J. Afghani), intellectually stifling *taqlīd* (M. Abduh), corruption (Anwar Ibrahim, Rachid Ghannouchi), and general decline (Muslim Brotherhood and Mawdudi's Jamaat-e Islami). Recently Tariq Ramadan wrote that "the Islamists of today have developed a conservative message, one that seeks only to adapt. The contemporary Muslim conscience must free itself from this message, and renew its commitment to the reformative and near-revolutionary power of the human and spiritual content of its tradition, which calls equally for reconciliation with self and openness to others."[10]

Reformism strives both to reconstruct the society in moral terms (*iṣlāḥ*) and to redefine and reinterpret major teachings of Islam (*tajdīd*). By combining socio-moral reconstruction and reconstruction of religious thought, reformists simultaneously aspire to change their environment and accept to be changed. In such a way, the often disturbing gap between Islamic ideals and social realities narrows down.

In some reformist movements, the reinterpretation aspect is emphasized while in others the social reform is in focus. In both cases reformist groups face disapproval from both the establishment, which tends to be accommodationist, and the general community, which tends to be conservative. The establishment is often disturbed by the social reform aspect of the reformist message while conservatives are annoyed by its *tajdīdī* spirit. In recent history, particularly brutal in this respect were several Arab regimes in the second half of the twentieth century (Egypt, Syria, Tunis, Iraq, and Libya).

Militant Extremism

From time to time the Muslim Community has witnessed the rise of radical nihilism or anarchism usually in the form of militants and terrorists of various kinds. They too want change, but one that implies destroying the society that exists and creating an idealized utopia. No such plan has ever succeeded in creating sustainable change.

Changing Criteria of Acceptable Change

What strikes one most in the context of our topic is the change that has been observed with regard to the standards and criteria of what is supposed to be unchangeable in the eyes of the Community. The common position used to be that anything that is based on uncontestable (qaṭ'ī) evidence, both in terms of its authenticity and definite meaning, is fixed. An example of that are Islamic norms of inheritance. To this criterion another, less precise standard is often added—the criterion of that "which is known of religion by necessity" (ma'lūm min al-dīn bi ḍarūra). While in this way the scope of unchangeable things is significantly reduced, it does not go far enough to enable change in understanding and interpretation of some contentious issues. Lately, however, more and more Muslim scholars have put forward "higher objectives of Sharī'ah" (maqāṣid al-sharī'ah) as the yardstick for what should be treated as unchangeable.[11] This is far from the common position of most 'ulamā' but nevertheless carries huge renewal potential. It enables a fresh look at all Islamic norms, including those based on qaṭ'ī evidence—such as inheritance—under the pretext that, while those norms stand for some other context, they are not meant to be applied in our context where they do not lead to the intended results.

The Arab Spring: A Case Study in Different Attitudes to Change

The Arab Spring that ensued following the self-immolation of the Tunisian street vendor Mohamed Bouazizi on December 17, 2010, is certainly the most dramatic change the Muslim world has seen recently. The reactions to this chain of events have varied significantly. Almost ironically, all those in power against whom the revolutions were directed hailed from the accommodationist trend in the Muslim Community, that is, from among those who should have least problem accepting the change. Their illiberalism obviously overruled their modernism. Somewhat more predictably, many traditional Muslim scholars and more conservative reformists (salafīs) sided with the established governments—or, at least, were not sure until quite late which side to take. A former Egyptian mufti proved to be one of the most reliable supporters of the Mubarak regime. Similarly, the late Syrian scholar M. S. R. al-Buti backed the Asad regime until his unfortunate death. Many Salafīs in Egypt consider their performance during the Egyptian revolution to be embarrassing. But whatever one may think, one has to admit that they were truthful to a well-established Sunnī tradition of loyalty to the authorities ('ulamā' al-sulṭa), whoever they may be (or almost so). Many people find the traditionalist assessment of the

Arab Spring bewildering, to say the least. While the views expressed in the popular publication *The 500 Most Influential Muslims* might not be shared by all traditionalists, they obviously are representative of a large section of this trend. In the introduction to the 2011 edition of this publication, the editor writes that the real heroes of change in Tunisia and Egypt were not street demonstrators but the army: "In neither Egypt nor Tunisia were the rulers overthrown by street demonstrators—in both cases it was the Army that decided to send off Ben Ali and Mubarak. In other words, the uprisings in Tunisia and Egypt did not overthrow the social or political order but were soft *coup d'états* that may or may not lead to reforms on one hand, or future blood baths on the other."[12]

The authors went on to praise the "non-politicized" army "as sacred warriors, as *mujahideen* in the traditional Islamic sense of armed struggle against the enemy at the frontier or criminal disorder in the streets." Applying the same approach, the volume itself estimates that the reformist figures, such as Y. al-Qaradawi, who supported the protests from the beginning are losers. Many others, however, think that liberal modernists and mainstream reformists are the movers and biggest winners of the Arab Spring. It seems that when traditionalists eventually had to concede to change, they tried to explain it in a way that will not counter their grand narrative, which prefers stability.[13]

And while it is too early to assess the Arab Spring's impact on Islamic political thinking, some reflections are justified. Like classical political thought, contemporary Islamic thinking has been ambiguous on issues of political change. Much Islamic political thinking suffers from false dichotomies: either stability and tyranny or anarchy and change, whereby tyranny always seemed to be a lesser evil. Hence comes the tendency of the scholars to side with the powers of the day. However, recent Arab revolutions have put this thinking and political culture to an unprecedented test. Many Islamic scholars performed poorly during the revolutions by siding with the old regimes, giving contradictory statements, or keeping silent. As a result, their credibility and authority have significantly depleted. The revolutions blasted away not only political leaders and regimes but also some religious ideas and leaders. Under certain conditions, stability is no more the value of highest order.

Overall the Arab Spring has had a humbling effect on many Muslim scholars and ideas. It has resulted in the demand for comprehensive revisions of certain interpretations of Islamic norms (e.g., Muhammad Hassan). Some have even called it "Ideational Revolution" and a "neglected duty" of today (e.g., Wail

Mirza). This is not to say that Islamic thought was not evolving prior to the revolutions, but the pace of change has accelerated since then and has included previously rarely debated issues, such as the transition of power.

This could be an important long-term consequence of the revolutions that we are just starting to observe. The Egyptian (and possibly Syrian) experience is of particular importance in this regard. The Arab Spring is an unprecedented opportunity for a major leap forward, not only in Arab political praxis but in Islamic political thinking as well. The question might even be whether the Arab Spring will influence the Sunnī Islamic political thinking to the extent that the Iranian Revolution altered the Shiʿī thought, or whether Traditionalist and Salafī Sunnī political thought will continue to simply follow political developments on the ground and justify them by selective quotations from Islamic sources—as they did during the Egyptian revolution—and miss this great opportunity altogether. Whatever the case, the reputation of these two groups has already suffered among the educated Muslims. (This might not be the case with all Muslims, as electoral success of Salafis in Egypt shows.) However, if instability continues for too long and takes too many lives and costs even more suffering, then it would not be difficult to imagine the reaffirmation of traditionalist and conservative positions on the issues of change.

Conclusion

Despite claims of Muslim and non-Muslim fundamentalists, both distant and recent histories provide ample evidence of the ability of Muslims and Islam to simultaneously change and ensure continuity. The great turbulence that we have been observing during the last century or so is nothing but a sign that a major reinterpretation of the great tradition of Islam is taking place.

The dust over the events of the Arab Spring has not settled yet, but the Islamic thinking on change and its desirability is evolving rapidly. Unless these events take a terribly wrong turn, future Muslim attitudes to change might be reasonably expected to be much more positive.

Notes

1. Yusuf Ali, *The Holy Qurʾān* (Beltsville, MD: Amana Publications, 1989). Pickthall's translation reads: "Lo! Allah changeth not the condition of a folk until they (first) change that which is in their hearts."

2. M. A. S. Abdel Haleem's translation of 13:11 reads: "God does not change the condition of a people [*for the worse*] unless they change what is in themselves." Emphasis added.

3. Wael Hallaq defends *taqlīd* among legal scholars at least as the only viable option in legal practice.

4. Muddathir Abd al-Rahim, "The Roots of Revolution in the Qur'an," *Dirasat Ifriqiyya* 3 (1987): 9–20; and Sayyid Abul A'la Maududi, *A Short History of the Revivalist Movement in Islam* (Petaling Jaya: Other Press, 1999).

5. John O. Voll, *Islam: Continuity and Change in the Muslim World*, 2nd ed. (Syracuse: Syracuse University Press, 1994), 21–22.

6. Here I am partially in agreement with the notions expressed by Voll in *Continuity and Change* (1994).

7. Qur'ān 56:12–14 says: "In Gardens of Bliss: *A number* of people from those of old, and *a few* from those of later times (*thullatun min al-awwalin wa qalilun min al-akhirin*)." Emphasis added.

8. Seyyed Hossein Nasr, "Decadence, Deviation and Renaissance in the Context of Contemporary Islam," in *Al-Huda* e-newsletter, June 2012, accessed August 31, 2013, www.al-huda.com/Article_7of130.htm.

9. Martin van Bruinessen, "Pesantren and kitab kuning: Continuity and Change in a Tradition of Religious Learning," in *Texts from the Islands: Oral and Written Traditions of Indonesia and the Malay World*, ed. Wolfgang Marschall (Berne: University of Berne Institute of Ethnology, 1994), 125.

10. Tariq Ramadan, "Beyond Islamism," August 5, 2013, http://tariqramadan.com/english/2013/08/05/beyond-islamism/.

11. Tariq Ramadan, *Radical Reform: Islamic Ethics and Liberation* (New York: Oxford University Press, 2009).

12. S. Abdallah Schleifer, ed., *The 500 Most Influential Muslims 2011* (Amman: Royal Islamic Strategic Studies Center, 2011), 4–8.

13. Imran Husain's interpretation of the developments unfolding in the Muslim world is even more puzzling. See, for instance, "Pax Islamika—Islamsko poimanje medunarodnog poretka od šejha Imrana Huseina," March 30, 2012, www.youtube.com/watch?v = U2f6Rlk KItk&feature = player_embedded.

The Christian Church Facing Itself and Facing the World

An Ecumenical Overview of Modern Christian Ecclesiology

BRANDON GALLAHER

Perhaps the major ecclesial, theological, and, indeed, ecumenical event of the twentieth century was Vatican II (1962–1965).[1] It provides a good starting point for any discussion of modern ecclesiology in all Christian churches because, as a council, it consulted widely with other Christian churches in the formulation of its ecclesiological statements as well as in some cases with other religions.[2] Furthermore, the sorts of issues it raised concerning the place and role of the Church in the modern world are relevant to not only Roman Catholicism but Orthodoxy and Protestantism.[3]

Vatican II was called by Pope St. John XXIII (1881–1963; pope, 1958–63; canonized in April 2014) to respond positively to modernity. It was hoped that the Council would contribute to solutions for the problems of the modern world through its offering up of the resources of the Christian Gospel on individual issues (e.g., human rights, the arms race, ecumenism, non-Christian religions, and religious freedom). Such a positive theological encounter and dialogue with modernity required the Catholic Church carefully bringing itself up to date in certain areas and the rearticulation of Christian teaching for a new age so that the relevance of the Christian message would become more apparent and presented more effectively in all areas of human activity in the world.[4] The Christian Church in the mid-twentieth century found itself in a world that, even then, was beginning to be acknowledged as a world that was "post-Christendom." The Church no longer could be taken to provide the cultural framework for the Western world's social life. As the great French Catholic theologian—himself a Council expert or *peritus* (he drafted more of its documents than any other person)—Yves Congar (1904–95) put it, the Church no longer carries "the world within herself like a pregnant mother."[5] What was required, he argued, was a "new style for her presence in the world" and in this

97

overview of modern ecclesiology we shall view various attempts to reenvision the place and vocation of the Church in the modern world not only in Roman Catholicism but also in Eastern Orthodoxy and Protestantism.[6]

Beginning with a discussion of Vatican II, despite it being a Roman Catholic ecumenical council, is helpful to unpack the continuities and sharp changes in modern ecclesiology in all Christian traditions not only because it was an ecumenical event but also because it was, as Karl Rahner (1904–84), another council theologian, observed, "in all of its sixteen constitutions, decrees and explanations it has been concerned with the Church . . . a Council of the Church about the Church, a Council in which all the themes discussed were ecclesiological ones; which concentrated upon ecclesiology as no previous Council had ever done."[7] Thus, since Vatican II was a council dedicated to the Church, we find many helpful ideas as well as distinctions that can illumine not only Catholic ecclesiology but also its Protestant and Orthodox counterparts. And here we want to turn to the first of these distinctions that shall provide the framework for our discussion. Cardinal Léon-Josef Suenens (1904–96) of Belgium, in a famous speech during the first session of the Council in December 1962, argued that the Council should be dedicated to the Church and produce one constitution on the Church that would look at the Church *ad intra* (looking inward) and *ad extra* (looking outward). In the first case, the Church's nature, structure, and missionary activity should be investigated. In the second case, one needed to look at the relationship of the Church to the world beyond it in dialogue with it showing interest, inter alia, in the human person, demography, social justice, the third world, hunger, preaching to the poor, and peace and war. Dialogue, for Suenens, was with both the faithful and the brothers "who are not yet visibly united with us," by which presumably he meant separated Christians, but, given Vatican II's later interest in dialoguing with other religions including Islam, this ambiguity is important.[8]

We shall do likewise in this exploration as a means of understanding the tension between continuity and reform in the Church. First we shall look at ecclesiology *ad intra* with what is, arguably, the most important modern current in ecclesiology, often called "communion ecclesiology," which proposes that the Church as the Body of Christ is a divine-human organism or "mystical Body" that comes to be through an event of communion focused on the celebration of the sacraments and, above all, the Eucharist. From there we shall turn to ecclesiology *ad extra* with Latin American liberation theology and, more briefly, an examination of the various "liberation" or "contextual" theologies it spawned, especially feminism and black theology. These theologies are understood as Christian responses not only to injustice but to a world where the status quo of Christendom is no longer taken for granted.

But before we turn to this program, let us look briefly at another helpful distinction for understanding modern ecclesiology that is taken from Vatican II—that is, the distinction between theology as *ressourcement* ("re-sourcing" or "renewal through return to the sources") and *aggiornamento* ("updating"). I hope this distinction will help us further in grasping the tension in the Church between the ideal of continuity and the need to reform the Church in order to keep it vital. Here it is said that the Council was concerned with *ressourcement* or a return to the key sources of the Christian tradition beginning with the Bible where the Christian Gospel is proclaimed definitively going through to the Christian Fathers who interpreted the Gospel Word with authority and finding its final expression and outworking in the Christian life in the liturgical tradition of worship.[9] It was believed that such a return to the basics of the Christian faith would result in a renewal of both theology and the Church more broadly. This French neologism is often applied to the loose-knit "school" of French theologians—figures like Congar, Henri de Lubac (1896–1991), and Jean Daniélou (1905–74)—who were called the *"la nouvelle théologie"* by their opponents. Many of these men would end up being *periti* (theological experts) during Vatican II and would play key roles in the drafting of its various statements. In the decades prior to the Council, these theologians looked to the resources of the Church's past, especially the Christian Fathers and schoolmen (e.g., Augustine, Gregory of Nyssa, Aquinas, and Bonaventure), in order to speak to its present situation in the modern world. They hoped that through drinking from the sources of Christian tradition the Church and its theology would be spiritually revived in the wake of the stale rationalism and authoritarianism of the Catholic scholastic manual tradition that had been ascendant since the eighteenth century.

Vatican II, as well as the various forms of liberation theology it later inspired, was responding to a situation where the Catholic Church since at least the early nineteenth century had become arguably stagnant and reactionary. It was caught up in a rather defensive response to a modern philosophy shaped by the legacy of Descartes and especially Kant. The Church as an institution became violently opposed to (and ultimately officially condemned) the rather loose-knit movement of Catholic Modernism and its use of historical-criticism for the Bible and promotion of doctrinal development.[10] To the Enlightenment ideal of obtaining eternal and universal knowledge through a form of reasoning that was itself not weighed down by historical contingencies, the Church, beginning roughly in the 1850s, responded with Neo-Scholasticism or Neo-Scholastic (or sometimes, Roman) theology, which was later referred to as "thomism of the strict observance."[11] Neo-Scholasticism as a "school" was primarily situated in Rome (though other centers included, for example, Mainz and Louvain) as it early on became the "official" Vatican/Church theology for several generations until it came to a rather quick demise following Vatican II, given that it was in many ways completely at odds with the spirit of openness to the world of that Council. Major early figures of Neo-Scholasticism in Rome included the Italian philosopher and scourge of Modernism Matteo Liberatore (1810–92); the German Jesuit theologian and philosopher Joseph Kleutgen (1811–83), who was a key figure in the articulation of the doctrine of papal infallibility of Vatican I (1869–70) as a drafter of *Pastor aeternus* (1870); and the Italian Dominican Tommaso Maria Zigliara (1833–93), who was the leading nineteenth-century Dominican of Aristotelian Scholasticism, a major architect of the Thomistic Revival, and author of an extremely popular antimodernist textbook, *Summa philosophica* (1876). Later figures, also based in Rome, include the Italian Jesuit Guido Mattiussi (1852–1925), who was an ardent opponent of what he believed was the "subjectivism" of Kant and Kantianism; the French Dominican Édouard Hugon (1867–1929), who wrote a widely circulated manual of scholastic philosophy; and, perhaps the best-known Neo-Scholastic thinker today, the French Dominican Scholastic Reginald Garrigou-Lagrange (1877–1964).[12] Garrigou-Lagrange, author of countless commentaries on Aquinas as well as numerous Neo-Scholastic tomes on everything from God and Mary to predestination and grace, was the doctoral supervisor of both Marie-Dominique Chenu (1895–1990), who would later be a key proponent in the historical study of Aquinas and opponent of Neo-Scholasticism (silenced for a period by Garrigou-Lagrange himself[13]) and then subsequently teacher of Congar and finally a key peritus at Vatican II; and Karol Wojtyla (1920–2005), that is, the future Pope St. John Paul II (pope, 1978–2005; canonized in April 2014), who wrote a doctorate under Garrigou-Lagrange on St. John of the Cross (1542–91).

Neo-Scholasticism was, arguably, less concerned with the propounding of the theology of Aquinas as such than with the putting forth of a counter-Enlightenment scholastic teaching that (at least initially) attempted to synthesize somewhat unstably the nominalist-tinged theology of a figure like the great

Spanish Jesuit scholastic Francisco Suárez (1548–1617) and the counter-Reformation Thomistic philosophy of Thomas Cajetan (1469–1534), known as the opponent of Martin Luther (1483–1546), producing an ahistorical rational systematization of Christian teaching that emphasized the immutability, infallibility, and objectivity of the Church's teaching and the necessity of achieving a correct balance of faith and reason. The Church's authoritative teaching or magisterium was expressed as a system of positive truths. It was designed to hold together as a sort of intricate clockwork mechanism that was rationally defensible in a syllogistic sense. This Neo-Scholastic version of the magisterium was supposed to be a sort of perennial theology existing in a pure, timeless world of truths that were themselves rationally provable beyond the flux of individual experience (modern philosophy was attacked as capitulating to subjectivism), historical events, the experience of particular communities and really any knowledge that might be achieved through empirical methods. This made those defending Neo-Scholasticism suspicious not only of most scientific developments but also of the application of these methods to the study of the development of doctrine and the evolution of the Bible as a text of texts. Neo-Scholasticism, which was expressed in rational manuals for the clergy (hence, talk of "manual theology" in reference to this theology by its opponents), was given official Church blessing by a long series of popes.

Neo-Scholasticism was enthroned, as it were, as the Church's official "school" of theology in the 1879 encyclical *Aeterni Patris* (itself drafted by both Zigliara and Kleutgen[14]) of Pope Leo XIII (1810–1903; pope, 1878–1903) that encouraged the development of a "Christian philosophy" to counter "secular philosophy" and the nascent Catholic Modernist movement with its appeal to Enlightenment ideals and drawing on the thought of such diverse figures as Descartes, Kant, and Hegel. The Enlightenment, it had been argued rather reductively by the Church establishment for decades prior to *Aeterni Patris*, emphasized universal human rights, the inviolability and freedom of the human conscience, the self-determination of particular nations and peoples with a unique ethnos, and the power of apparently irrefutable scientific discoveries. Thus, Blessed Pope Pius IX (1792–1878; pope, 1846–78; beatified, 2000), for example, condemned key elements of liberal democracy in his encyclical *Quanta cura* (1864), including what he called political "naturalism," or the teaching that civil society should be governed without any particular attention to religion, whether true or false; that all men had a right to free speech and liberty of conscience; and communism and socialism, or the teaching that domestic society or the family borrows its whole reason for being from civil law alone and that the rights of parents over their children (for education and care) only emanate from civil law.[15] More famously, as an appendix to *Quanta cura*, Pius IX also promulgated his now infamous *Syllabus of Errors* (1864), which was a list of condemned propositions or "modern errors" ranging from pantheism, naturalism, and absolute rationalism to sundry errors concerning the limitation of the civil power of the pope (essentially further hemming in his civil power in the then much diminished Papal States) and those concerning "modern liberalism" (e.g., that it is no longer expedient that Catholicism be the only religion of the state to the exclusion of all other cults whatsoever).[16] The Church further responded to what it regarded as the threats of the modern age at Vatican I in 1870 with the affirmation in the Dogmatic Constitution on the Church, *Pastor aeternus* (drafted by Kleutgen along with the Constitution on the Catholic Faith, *Dei filius*), that it alone was the bastion of infallible truth and unerring teachings expressed in particular carefully delimited momentous positive statements by the pope that were deemed infallible and did not require the consensus of the Church.[17]

All of this rather reactionary culture was one where the "Church" as the "Body of Christ" gradually became indistinguishable from the hierarchy, above all the papacy, and its official teaching or magisterium. The Church's divinization of its own authority, reactionary critique of Modernism, and elevation of one theological school as its official spokesmen culminated in a series of ecclesiastical actions in the early twentieth century that in their excessive overreaching of ecclesial power and centralization could not but lead to a "backlash" of sorts. This backlash came with Vatican II's openness and embrace of the modern world as well as the strong emphasis on conciliarity and the fact that the Church was not only characterized by papal authority and hierarchy but was above all a "holy People of God" that included the laity. In 1907 Pope St. Pius X (1835–1914; pope, 1903–14; canonized in 1954) officially condemned Catholic Modernism's use of historical-criticism for the Bible and advocacy of doctrinal development, thus putting an official stamp on the disapproval of the Church of reform movements keen on dialoguing with modernity.[18] In the next seven years Neo-Scholasticism "locked-in," as it were, its ascendency. This included the introduction in 1910 of an antimodernist clerical oath (with the threat of excommunication) required of all bishops, priests, and teachers, which was not abolished until Venerable Pope Paul VI (1897–1978; pope, 1963–68; declared "venerable" or a person "heroic in virtue" by Pope Benedict XVI in December

2012; and he is to be beatified by Pope Francis in October 2014) did so several years after the close of Vatican II in 1967.[19] Clerical education, by canon law, required candidates to attend Latin lectures in philosophy for three years given by professors propounding the method, doctrine, and principles of Aquinas following the Neo-Scholastic interpretation. Students were then required to undergo official examinations (also in Latin) before sitting through a further four years of theology instruction, also in Latin and following Neo-Scholastic principles.[20] These philosophy examinations, beginning in 1914, were required by decree to be framed after the "Twenty-Four Thomistic Theses" (drafted by Mattiussi and Hugon) that aimed to instill in the pupil the true Church teaching on ontology, cosmology, psychology, and theodicy.[21] The effect on students was more often than not less than salutary, and the great Roman Catholic systematic theologian Hans Urs von Balthasar (1905–88), who suffered through these mandatory lectures on philosophy as a Jesuit novice, described himself at the time as "languishing in the desert of neo-scholasticism."[22] The wave of Roman Neo-Scholastic antimodernism paralyzed the Catholic Church well into the 1960s, and, indeed, many of the key figures at Vatican II (e.g., Chenu, Congar, de Lubac, and Rahner) were at different times under censure or investigation by the "doctrinal watch-dog," the Supreme Sacred Congregation of the Holy Office (from 1985, the Congregation for the Doctrine of the Faith [CDF]) of the Roman Curia.[23] Indeed, rather humorously, Rahner was under investigation by the Holy Office right up until shortly after he was called as a *peritus* for the forthcoming Second Vatican Council, at which point the investigation was suddenly dropped![24]

Returning to our main subject, *ressourcement* as an idea also can be broadly be applied to the Orthodox theological movement in the twentieth century—including Myrrha Lot-Borodine (1882–1957), Georges Florovsky (1893–1979), Vladimir Lossky (1903–58), and John Zizioulas (b. 1931)—called "neo-patristic synthesis" (a phrase of Georges Florovsky) that wished to return to the Eastern patristic and liturgical sources of Orthodox tradition in order to renew the Orthodox Church and its theology by returning to a tradition that was not distorted by successive waves of Westernization in the Christian East.[25] And let us go further and venture that it can be applied to the work of Karl Barth (1996–68) and the broad-based movement of Protestant "Neo-Orthodoxy" with its break with the nineteenth-century Protestant Liberal collapse of culture and Christianity.[26] This cultural collapse can be seen, for example, in the German theological establishment's support of the Kaiser and the Fatherland in

World War I in the 1914 "Manifesto of the 93" German intellectuals, which "betrayal" led Barth to his decisive critique of German liberal Protestantism. Neo-Orthodoxy emphasized (in contrast to the culturally determined "religion" of liberal Protestantism), among other things, the transcendence of God while simultaneously upholding the existential nature of faith, that the event of divine revelation was given in the Word of God, Jesus Christ, as proclaimed in scripture, and that there needed to be a renewed attention to the magisterial Reformers, especially Calvin and Luther. In order to articulate the nature and structure of the Church in the context of the new challenges of modernity and to enter into dialogue with the world in regard to all aspects of human life, Christian theologians of all churches in the twentieth century drank deeply of the wellsprings of Christian tradition as they believed that only through such a resourcing could theology properly articulate this new moment for the Church.

But this brings us to the idea of *aggiornamento*, which is an Italian term including in it the term *giorno*, or "day," and meaning "updating," "revision," "renovation," "modernization," and even "reform."[27] It was a term much favored by John XXIII in reference to his vision for Vatican II.[28] He held that since the Church was a dynamic and living divine-human organism, she could adapt, renew, renovate, and even at times perhaps reform some of the changing historical aspects of her life as the modern times necessitated without ceasing to be the self-same Body because her underlying essence remained the same. This is well summed up by the famous quote attributed to "Good Pope John" (as John XXIII is frequently called): "I want to throw open the windows to the Church so that we can see out and people can see in." In commenting in October 2012 on the fiftieth anniversary of the start of Vatican II, Pope Emeritus Benedict XVI (Joseph Ratzinger, b. 1927; pope, 2005–13) observed that Pope John XXIII was right to use the term *aggiornamento* for the growth and development of the Church in Vatican II, despite the objections of some. Pope John's "true intuition," Benedict argues, is that Christianity is ever ancient and ever new, and it lives from the eternal today of the God who entered into space and time and is present in all times. It is a tree that is ever new and timely such that with the Church's updating of itself, as in Vatican II, it does not break with tradition and simply change with the fashion of the times. The "updating" of the Church in Vatican II, therefore, was not an updating that reflected what pleased random Council Fathers and the public opinion of the day, but it had a theological rationale of grounding all ecclesial changes in the eternal life of God: "we must bring the 'today' that we live to the standard of the Christian event, we must bring the 'today' of our time to the 'today' of God." Vatican II, as is the case with the Church throughout all history, must speak to the people of today and bring God's eternal today into the today of the people of our time, but it can only do this and remain self-same by being grounded in God and the tradition of His Church and being guided by Him in living out their faith with purity.[29] Concrete examples of this attempt of the Catholic Church to update her own life range from the nearly unprecedented texts from Vatican II encouraging religious freedom, ecumenism, and dialogue with non-Christian religions to the introduction in the decades following the Council of liturgy in the vernacular, the celebration of the mass facing the people, and greater lay participation.[30] But, more controversially, some would argue that Protestant churches have renewed and updated the Church's life by the encouragement of women's ministries since the rise of the women's liberation movement in the late 1960s. Going yet further with this same line of thinking, in the late twentieth to early twenty-first centuries, the argument is made that *aggiornamento* can also be seen in the well-publicized attempts by many churches to include the voices and gifts of lesbian, gay, bisexual, and transgendered (LGBT) persons within the totality of the witness to the world of the gospel by Christ's Body.

The Orthodox, arguably, have yet to meet their moment of *aggiornamento*. Much of recent Eastern Orthodox history has been taken up with either de-Westernization or persecution (e.g., the Soviet Union), so there has been little space available for a decisive encounter with modernity. Nevertheless, some theologians would point to (somewhat ambivalent) recent attempts to respond to human rights, secularism, and bioethical issues as examples of Orthodox *aggiornamento*.[31] Thus, the search for an Eastern Orthodox creative response to a (post-) modernity that yet remains faithful to traditional faith and practice and avoids the temptation (as seen in some churches in the West) to jettison the apparently archaic forms of the past in favor of the "new" and "relevant" forms of this present age of the world is one of the central tasks of contemporary Orthodox theology.

This task may be accomplished sooner rather than later. In March 2014 the primates or leading bishops of the local churches making up the Orthodox Church gathered in Istanbul (historically called "Constantinople" for the Orthodox) for a "synaxis" or major ecclesial gathering. They announced that a "Holy and Great Synod" (i.e., Church Council) would be convened by Ecumenical Patriarch Bartholomew of Constantinople–New Rome for the summer of 2016 in Istanbul/Constantinople. The meeting is to be held in the historic church Hagia Eirene, which was the site of the Second Ecumenical Council in 381. The Ecumenical Patriarch is traditionally *primus inter pares,* or first among equals of all the leaders of the Orthodox Church. The 2016 Synod/Council would be presided over by the Ecumenical Patriarch and his brother primates of the Other Autochephalous (i.e., self-headed or independent) Churches would be seated on his right and his left.[32] This liturgical order is "iconic" and meant to image the Church in the form of Christ surrounded by his disciples. The last time the Orthodox had a Pan-Orthodox council of this scale was in 879–880 (though not deemed "ecumenical" subsequently), and it dealt with the addition of the *filioque* to the Nicene-Constantinopolitan creed and reinstated Photios I (ca. 810–ca. 893) to the patriarchal throne of Constantinople. The last (Seventh) Ecumenical Council for the Orthodox was in 787 in Nicaea. Some are already, perhaps precipitously, referring to this upcoming event as the "Eighth Ecumenical Council." This 2016 event has been in the discussion and then planning stage since a pan-Orthodox meeting in Istanbul in 1923 with a particularly active phase of successive meetings in the 1960s. An Inter-Orthodox Preconciliar Commission that is charged with preparing the Council's agenda has been meeting since the late 1970s with its last major gathering in 2009.[33] Thus, the next Orthodox (Ecumenical) Council is much expected, and there is also much doubt as to whether it will actually come to pass. It is somewhat (as is frequently joked) like the Second Coming of Christ. Indeed, the Primates' statement of March 2014 said the council would be convened in 2016 "unless something unexpected occurs."[34]

It is hoped by some contemporary theologians that this 2016 event will seize the day and respond positively to modernity—somewhat akin to the Roman Catholic Vatican II—putting forward a vision of Orthodoxy that speaks proactively to not only a post-Byzantine order but a post-Christian pluralistic and secular world. This would provide a sure basis for ongoing local adaptations of sundry ancient Orthodox liturgical and sacramental practices according to present modern needs as well as nascent attempts to respond to new developments from bioethical dilemmas to religious pluralism. Indeed, in October 2014 there will be a meeting devoted to just such a vision of the council. Thirty of the leading Orthodox academic theologians, led by professors Aristotle Papanikolaou and George Demacopoulos of Fordham University's Orthodox Christian Studies Center, will gather in New York to discuss the forthcoming council and their hopes and concerns about it. A second part to this October 2014 meeting is planned for the spring of 2015 with possible episcopal participants. However, at best—and this is even in doubt, given that all the future council's decisions will be by the consensus of all the local churches (each of which gets one vote)[35]—this 2016 council will only respond to the current crisis of disorder in the Orthodox "diaspora" (all those ecclesial territories outside traditional canonical borders of the local churches: for example, the Orthodox churches in North and South America). The present order in the diaspora is a cacophony of overlapping ethnic Orthodox jurisdictions where (contradictory to Orthodox ecclesiology) there is more than one bishop per city and the primacy of Constantinople is routinely contested. But even if a resolution of the disunity of the Orthodox Church was all that was accomplished by this council, this would be an enormous achievement given Orthodoxy's noncentralized polity, great age, and resistance to change. A more unified Orthodoxy would be an Orthodoxy prepared for the future and ready to face the challenges of change instead of acting like history stopped in 1453 with the fall of Constantinople to the Ottomans and the disintegration of the Byzantine Empire. One must, therefore, hope that the Orthodox bishops will listen to the promptings of the Spirit and put the Church's house in order. Therefore, in each of the major Christian traditions, Roman Catholicism, Protestantism, and Orthodoxy, we see the continual Christian tension between maintaining continuity with tradition and the bedrock of one's life and a movement toward a response or even a reform of the Body so that it can remain relevant and ever vital to each generation to which the Christian Gospel is proclaimed.

Part I: Ecclesiology *Ad intra*

In order to understand the immensely influential trend of "communion ecclesiology," our example of an *ecclesiology ad intra*, we must turn to its "father." While discussing John XXIII's idea of *aggiornamento*, we brought up the idea of the Church as a divine-human "organism," a living mystical Body. As a variant of the Biblical image or model of the Church as the Body of Christ (1 Cor. 12: 12–14), the Church as a divine-human organism is a key metaphor of modern ecclesiology. The roots of the metaphor are patristic and medieval, but it was revived through the re-sourcing theological work of Johann Adam Möhler (1796–1838) of the Catholic Tübingen School. In his immensely influential *Unity in the Church or The Principle of Catholicism Presented in the Spirit of the Church Fathers of the First Three Centuries* (1825), Möhler draws on a wide number of Church Fathers to articulate through the lens of Romanticism a vision of the living Body of Christ. The Spirit of Christ is the "life-giving and life-forming principle" that animates the Body of Christ as the fullness of all believers in Him who together comprise a spiritual unity. In being filled by the Spirit of Christ, the Church, as the "totality of believers that the Spirit forms, is the unconquerable treasure of the new life principle, ever renewing and rejuvenating herself, the uncreated source of nourishment for all."[36] The Church as a "living organism" is understood as the "external, visible structure of a holy living power, of love, the body of the spirit of believers forming itself from the interior externally." Thus the divine Spirit here manifests itself as an external divine-human organism living in individual Christians through which it perpetuates true faith and love in God.[37] The Church, Möhler would argue later in the more self-consciously "orthodox" and Christocentric *Symbolism* (1843), is—adapting a common counter-Reformation notion—a visible society of men founded by Christ, which expresses outwardly and in a continuing fashion in history the divine Word, which took flesh. It is then both a human reality, an institution in which the spirit of Christ continues to work and His word continues to resound, but it is also a divine reality. It is divine insofar as it is a permanent manifestation of the spirit of Christ. In short, the Church is a divine-human organism through which the incarnation is extended in history: "Thus the visible Church . . . is the Son of God himself everlastingly manifesting himself among men in a human form, perpetually renewed and eternally young—the enduring incarnation of the same, as in Holy Scriptures, even the faithful are called the 'Body of Christ.' "[38]

The Spirit rules in that Body by begetting orders, organs. and functions (e.g., the Church hierarchy) for the Body through which the Body expresses itself and preserves an inner unity of life, binding everything together internally and working externally.[39] Möhler strongly emphasizes, following 1 Peter 2:9, that all believers have a "priestly dignity" as they all participate in the priestly office of Christ, though this in no way negates the ordained priest who is a "synecdoche of all believers because he expresses their unity."[40] But how does the Spirit communicate itself and its unity to believers? While Möhler mostly takes this for granted, and it is not the central focus of his theology in the way that it will be for later communion ecclesiologists building on his thought, he is explicit that it is by the Eucharist that Christ "binds himself to us in a living, real, and substantial way."[41] The spiritual unity of the Body of Christ, particularly expressed in the Eucharist, has a definite institutional shape as the Body is an "ecclesiastical organism."[42] Thus, Möhler describes successively unity in the bishop, the metropolitan, the total episcopate or college of bishops, and the primate, which for him is the pope.[43] The bishop, in heading the Eucharistic community and eventually (as the Church grew larger) the diocese, is the union of believers made visible in a specific place, their love made personal, and "the manifestation and living center point of the Christian disposition striving towards unity."[44] But the unity of the Body only ever increases for Möhler, and if the bishop is the center of the diocese, then the metropolitan is the center around which a gathering of bishops in communion come together and their respective gathered communities. What is still needed is a representation of the unity of all the bishops as a "living image," and here we have the pope or primate of the one Church of all believers understood as "the living center of the living unity of the whole Church."[45]

Now it cannot be emphasized strongly enough how influential Möhler's nascent "communion ecclesiology" has been in modern theology.[46] Alongside the ecclesiology of Friedrich Schleiermacher (1768–1834), to which we shall later turn, it is, as Roger Haight has argued, the strongest representation of modern ecclesiology.[47] Though we shall not elaborate this for want of space, communion ecclesiology now forms the common ecclesiology of the official ecumenical movement as expressed in such texts of the Faith and Order Commission of the World Council of Churches as the now-famous *Baptism, Eucharist, Ministry* (1983)—of which Wolfhart Pannenberg and Jean-Marie Tillard were principle drafters—and, recently, *The Church: Towards a Common Vision* (2013).[48] We shall now trace in Roman Catholicism, Orthodoxy, and Protestantism some developments of Möhler's ideas.

In Roman Catholicism, the idea of the Church as a divine-human organism leads quite naturally to seeing the Church as a "sacrament" and the "mystical Body of Christ," and, after Möhler, we see these themes taken up by individual theologians as well as in official Church statements. Thus we see both themes come together in the early twentieth century in the work of the excommunicated Catholic Modernist writer and Irish Jesuit priest George Tyrrell (1861–1909). Tyrrell held that the Church was the "mystical Body of Christ" animated by the Spirit through which we are brought into direct contact with the "ever present Christ" who is heard in the gospel and touched in the sacraments. Christ, following Möhler, lives on in the Church "not metaphorically but actually," through which "instrument" the force of His Spirit "is transmitted and felt": "The Church is not merely a society or school, but a mystery and sacrament; like the humanity of Christ of which it is an extension."[49]

Tyrrell was not alone in drawing on Möhler, for we see his influence even more strongly in Congar who, under the direction of Chenu, completed lectoral and doctoral degrees at the Dominican Studium Le Saulchoir, Belgium, on the unity of the Church in Möhler's theology. Indeed, he began a French translation project of *Unity in the Church*, which he finally published in 1938. For Congar, Möhler's organicist vision of the unity of the Church becomes a sort of mysticism of Christ's Body binding us ever closer to Him in faith and charity.[50] The Church, for Congar, is an organism insofar as it is a Body having different functions where each part is "animated" in view of its own being as it performs its special task to the benefit of the whole. The idea of the Church as an organism is helpful in understanding the respective roles of the faithful and the hierarchy. The whole Body, all believers, is animated by the Spirit, and within it the hierarchical functions of service and those who exercise them are animated and exercised for this purpose.[51] Like Möhler again, Congar emphasized the sacerdotal or priestly character of the laity or the assembled believers, who are the very members comprising the mystical Body or divine-human organism of Christ. They share in Christ's threefold office of priest, king, and prophet.[52]

But to speak of the Church in this way is to equate it with the "mystical Body of Christ."[53] From start to finish, for Congar, the actualization of this Body in human beings is a gift of Christ to man by which He prolongs and continues Himself in humanity, recreating that humanity in Himself after the image of God. In union with the Body of Christ, the Christian acts and leads a life whose true principle is Christ. He sees and judges after Christ, whose life and vision becomes his very own. This is the "realization of the Mystical Body, of a life led on Christ's account" understood as being living members of His Body united in faith and love in Him through which He continues His life in us.[54] The function of the sacraments, for Congar, is that they realize this mystical union with Christ in His Body—that is, they mediate Christ to us insofar as they are, like the Church itself, "a prolongation of the incarnation of the Word." The Eucharist is exemplary here, as it is said to take us "deeper still" into "incorporation with Christ."[55]

Congar's close colleague and fellow *peritus* at Vatican II, Henri de Lubac, devoted his famous study, *Corpus mysticum* (1949; but finished 1938–39), to looking at the patristic and especially medieval roots lying behind the idea of the "mystical Body." In particular, de Lubac is concerned with how precisely the Eucharist is the "mystical principle" by which the ecclesial body becomes in all reality the Body of Christ. The Eucharist, the Body and Blood of Christ, is, he says, the "ever-springing source of life" of the one Spirit, which, when it is consumed by Christ's faithful people, makes them into one single Body. In the famous words of de Lubac, "the Eucharist makes the Church. It makes of it an inner reality. By its hidden power, the members of the body come to unite themselves by becoming more fully members of Christ, and their unity with one another is part and parcel of their unity with the one single Head."[56]

The Catholic Church begins to make this sort of communion ecclesiology part of its official teaching quite gradually. By the close of World War II, with the papal encyclical *Mystici Corporis Christi* (1943) of Ven. Pope Pius XII (1876–1958; pope, 1939–58; declared "Venerable" by Pope Benedict XVI in December 2009) (although generally now said to be drafted by the Dutch Jesuit and Curial theologian Sebastian Tromp [1889–1975]), we see the papal elaboration of the "Mystical Body of Christ, which is the Church" and which we are told "was first taught us by the Redeemer Himself."[57] The Body is now completely collapsed with the institution of the Roman Catholic Church: "this true Church of Jesus Christ—which is the One, Holy, Catholic, Apostolic and Roman Church [*hanc veracem Christi Ecclesiam—quae sancta, catholica, apostolica, Romana Ecclesia est*]—we shall find nothing more noble, more sublime, or more divine than the expression 'the Mystical Body of Christ.' "[58] This would seem to leave all those who are not under the Roman pontiff out in the cold, as there is a direct identity here between Rome and the "mystical Body of the Redeemer," but Pius XII feels that during a time of war the message of the "divine given unity" of the mystical Body joining all races and peoples is all the more important, and that those outside the walls of the Church "will be forced to admire this fellowship in charity, and with the guidance and assistance of divine grace will long to share in the same union and charity."[59] They have, he opines, in this way of admiration of the Church a relationship to her by "unconscious desire and longing," and he waits for them "with open and outstretched arms to come not to a stranger's house, but to their own, their father's home."[60]

With Vatican II we see the theology of Möhler come fully into the mainstream with the Dogmatic Constitution on the Church, *Lumen Gentium* (1964). Indeed, this document, as well as so many others produced by Vatican II, so completely expressed communion ecclesiology that the 1985 Extraordinary Catholic Synod of Bishops described it as the "central and fundamental idea of the Council's Document's."[61] It is not surprising, then, that we see Möhlerean ecclesiology at Vatican II as Congar had a hand in drafting large portions of *Lumen Gentium* and Möhler himself was being read during the drafting process, as we know from Congar that Pope Paul VI asked him in the last stages for a copy of *Unity in the Church*.[62] Without rehashing all the aspects of communion ecclesiology in *Lumen Gentium* we can simply note that it contains all the characteristics of this theology including a belief that the Eucharist makes the Church (*Lumen Gentium*, I, 3), an emphasis (without in any way negating the hierarchy or the Roman pontiff: III) on the holy laity or the Church as the "People of God" (II and IV), who themselves were "a chosen race, a royal priesthood, a holy nation" (1 Pet. 2:9 cited at II, 9) (note the contrast with the older vision of the Church as being primarily the pope with *his* bishops and *his* presbyterium), a vision of the hierarchy and the priesthood as ministerial functions of the Eucharistic assembly of the said holy People of God (III), the Church as a sacrament (I, 1), the mystical Body of Christ (1, 8) (although direct talk of the Church as an "organism" is only found in *Gaudium et Spes*, Part II, 5.II.90[63]) as well as adding a new interesting eschatological vision of the Church (VII). More particularly, *Lumen Gentium* begins with a discussion of the mystery of the Church and quickly identifies the Church with "a sacrament or as a sign and instrument" not merely of creating a unity of believers but "both of a very closely knit union with God and of the unity of the whole human race" since the Church is a reality that desires to unfold its nature and mission not only to the faithful but the whole of creation (I, 1). We now take for granted this sort of sacramental language about the Church, but it was controversial in its day. Indeed, Congar tells us that one conservative bishop objected to the Church being spoken of as a sacrament because this sort of language had been used by the condemned (and then long dead) Modernist heretic Tyrrell![64] Further on in *Lumen Gentium*, we see the Church identified with the mystical Body. However, unlike earlier in Pius XII's encyclical, the Church does not exist in a simple identity with the Roman Catholic Church but it is said (in words whose meaning is debated to this day) that it "subsists in the Catholic Church" (*subsistit in Ecclesia catholica*) (I,8).[65] Later we are told that those who have not received the gospel are related "in various ways" to the People of God. The Jews are related to the Church through the Old Testament, the promises, and the fact that Christ was a Jew. The Muslims are related due to the fact that they acknowledge the Creator as they profess the faith of Abraham and worship with Christians the one God who will judge all on the last day. Providence in its wisdom guides all those not part of the Church to the gospel, and so with "care and attention" the Church encourages mission following the command of Christ (Mk. 6:16) (*Lumen Gentium*, II, 16).

These sorts of ambiguities, especially that of the meaning of the Roman Church "*subsistit in*" *Una Sancta* or Universal Christian Church, have caused much controversy in subsequent Catholic theology as well as official teaching because they were taken as a theological opportunity of sorts by some theologians interested in thinking about how not only non-Catholic Christians might be a part of the Church in some sense but also those of other faiths (and none[66]) might be included in a fashion.[67] Rahner is illustrative in this regard, as his famous theology of "anonymous Christianity" straddled the Council and was embellished subsequently.[68] He argues that, because Christ took flesh, humanity in advance was sanctified by grace and considered as a unity to be "the people of the children of God," a sort of proto- or ur-Church. With the coming of the Spirit after the Ascension, mankind is organized juridically and socially into the supernatural unity of "the Church" proper.[69] The world belongs to the Church merely with its heart (*corde*) but does not have the grace of being united to it bodily (*corpore*). This grace is essential for a human being to contribute to the basic sacramental sign, which is the Church, although it powers history forward to the eschaton or last things and is incarnate in history "in full measure and in manifest form" in Christ, though it has "all along been at work at the very roots of human nature as the offering of God to communicate himself to man regardless of whether this offering is accepted or refused."[70]

A similar attempt to appropriate the communion ecclesiology of *Lumen Gentium* for the purposes of a communion with non-Christians is found in the Dominican theologian and ecumenist Jean-Marie Tillard (1927–2000). He argues that the Church is born on Pentecost by a dynamism that recreates the flesh of the world. The Spirit has the power to tear this flesh from the sin and injustice that besets it, as the Spirit knows how to break down the walls that imprison individuals and groups from one another so that It might "bind them together in *communion*. For humanity is truly itself only in communion. This is what saves it."[71] The Church then is impelled from its origins to become involved in the world's problems from the very basis of its life in union with Christ through the Spirit. He acknowledges that the Church is the place where the "humanity-that-God-wills" is recreated in the event of loving communion through the Spirit uniting us with Christ.[72] However, there still exist some who are saved but ignorant of the fact that they are—though we would not call these "anonymous Christians" (following Rahner), because to be a Christian is to openly confess Jesus Christ as the source of salvation. These people, Tillard argues, belong to the *"communion* of grace." Moreover, because God acts in creation through His two hands, the Word, and the Spirit (Irenaeus), and in the Resurrection Jesus is made Lord of Creation, we must say that communion is a more universal reality than that manifested within the canonical walls of the Church as an institution. He says that all human beings are invited to communion who are true to their conscience and humble as well as those who worship God and are faithful to their religion or are united spiritually with their own faith. In a world where deferral to the transcendent is denied and mocked, a union happens between believers of different faiths who are alike reviled. Thus, when one experiences the sight of a Muslim making his "prayer ritual" under the sarcastic smiles of observers, then "one feels oneself instinctively affected by this derision. On a profound plane this man at prayer and we become one."[73]

Yet Catholicism was not alone in its development of the insights of Möhler. Orthodoxy early on drew creatively on his thought, as can be found especially in the work of the Slavophile Russian poet, philosopher, and theologian Aleksei Khomiakov (1804–60).[74] Khomiakov characteristically refers to the Church as a "living organism" that is animated by the divine spirit of truth, grace, and "mutual love" as the Savior lives in us, His Body making us an "organic unity in Jesus Christ."[75] This inner unity of the Spirit of the Church's members is made manifest externally in sacramental communion and, in particular, "bodily communion with its Savior" in the Eucharist.[76] This much is fairly standard fare for communion ecclesiology, but Khomiakov adds a new element, which is that he characterizes the unity of the Church as *sobornost* or catholicity (using the Slavonic word of the Creed *sobornyi* for the Greek *katholikos*: One Holy, Catholic, and Apostolic Church), and this he defines as a "free unanimity" of all in one and one in all (unity in plurality) allowing for the particularity of different peoples but also seeing this particularity as precisely reflecting the catholicity or universality of the Church.[77] The point is unfortunately couched in some fairly typical nineteenth-century interchurch polemics. He argues that Roman Catholicism or "Romanism," as he puts it, has merely an external unity that rejects freedom and so is a false unity, while Protestantism has an external freedom that does not bestow unity and so has a false freedom. Orthodoxy, being a sort of *via media*, incarnates the mystery of the unity of Christ and His elect, which is a unity actualized by His human freedom and which is revealed in the Church to be "the real unity and real freedom of the faithful."[78] Although this polemical framing is regrettable, the idea is original and will later prove important in Orthodox theology where the Spirit will become identified with freedom in diversity expressed in worship. Thus, Khomiakov argues, that unity is generated by freedom understood as the "moral law of mutual love and prayer," which is by the grace of God and not impelled from above as in an institution. In this spiritual free unity, all of the members of the Church from layman to bishop equally cooperate and participate in the "common work" of right praise in the liturgy.[79] Because Khomiakov argues that the unity of the Church is an interior reality of a free act of mutual love manifested externally in the Eucharist, this makes him agnostic regarding the limits of the Church. He tells us that the "secret bonds" that unite the earthly Church to the rest of humanity are not revealed to us, so one simply cannot condemn severely those outside her visible bounds as this contradicts divine mercy and because Christ is a "law" and "realized idea" imprinted in creation. Therefore, those who love justice, compassion, charity, love, sacrifice, and "all that is truly human, great, and beautiful, all that is worthy of respect, imitation, or adoration—all this represents only different forms of the name of our Savior."[80]

It is arguable that communion ecclesiology would not have its singular Eucharistic focus if it were not for the work of the seminal Russian émigré historian and theologian Nicholas Afanasiev (1893–1966).[81] Afanasiev's "Eucharistic ecclesiology" (communion ecclesiology is often referred to in this manner), which has since been developed by the Greek theologian John Zizioulas and has become massively influential, is summarized in a line from Afanasiev's famous 1960 essay (cited in the debates at Vatican II), "The Church That Presides in Love": "Where the Eucharist is, there is the fullness of the Church." What is not often mentioned is the next line, where he says the principle must be reversed, which is that where the fullness of the Church is not, there no Eucharist can be celebrated.[82] In other words, Church and Eucharist become, as we saw with his younger Catholic contemporaries Congar and de Lubac, two ways of speaking about the Church as the Body of Christ into which we as members are incorporated. Afanasiev argues that Christians are a priestly people of the one high priest, Jesus Christ, who, in gathering together in one assembly in one city, manifest in and around their one bishop the unity and fullness (namely, catholicity) of the Church of God.[83] Each local church—in communion with all local churches—is simultaneously fully catholic, universal through the Holy Spirit's animation of its gratitude to God (*eucharistia*), its diversification by the fullness of the gifts poured out on each person, and as Christ dwells in it through the Eucharist by which the faithful through communication become members of His Body.[84] Thus, the "Church of God in Christ" is one although it is made manifest in a multitude of local churches, each of which has the fullness of God because it is a Eucharistic gathering.[85] All ecclesial ministries or offices (deacon, priest, and bishop), which are understood in terms of "service" (reminiscent of Congar[86]), as well as their order and function originate from the Eucharistic assembly of each local Church.[87] Following Khomiakov, Catholicity—and, with it, unity—is defined as a realization of the Spirit ("The beginning of the Church lies in the Spirit. Through the Spirit and in the Spirit the Church lives"[88]) and is grounded once again in the Eucharistic assembly so that Afanasiev (controversially) identifies all attempts to erect "universal" ecclesial structures beyond the local assembly and its presbyter-bishop (as the two offices blur in earliest Christianity) with the slow triumph of law over the power of love (*vlast' liubvi*).[89] Here Afanasiev was influenced by a Lutheran opposition of law and grace in his reaction to, among other things, Caesaro-papism, Roman Catholic papalist "universal ecclesiology," and the overlapping jurisdictions of the Russian diaspora in his day.[90] He nevertheless argued, a fact sometimes forgotten, for Roman "primacy," which he understood as its "priority" as a local Church that presides over others in love (echoing Ignatius of Antioch).[91]

Our last Orthodox figure, John Zizioulas (titular Metropolitan of Pergamon under the Ecumenical Patriarchate), is perhaps the best-known exponent of "communion ecclesiology," and (arguably) one of the most celebrated living theologians in Christian East and West.[92] His importance as a thinker comes from emphasizing that ecclesiology must be based on a combination of Trinitarian theology and Christology if it is to be an ecclesiology of communion. These doctrines are "indispensable presuppositions" for a communion ecclesiology. It must be based on Trinitarian theology in that God is a communion (*koinonia*) of persons, relational in His very being, and the Church's being is likewise relational. It must also be based on Christology in that Christ is the head of His Body, the Church, and He is a corporate Pneumatological or Spiritual Being "born and existing in the *koinonia* of the Spirit."[93] The Church's identity derives from her relationship with the Triune God insofar as she must reflect His being, which is one of personal communion, as well as enter into communion with Him via continual incorporation and personalization through sacramental participation in His Spiritual Body, the Church.[94]

Moreover, Zizioulas argues, within a vision of ecclesiology drawn from the Greek patristic corpus and Byzantine liturgical tradition, the very structures, ministries, vision of authority, mission, and understanding of Tradition of the

Church must be relational, reflecting the life of God as Trinity. Thus, how the bishop connects with his flock in a ministry of unifying diversity is relational just as the relationship of dioceses on the universal level, which are integrated through the unity of the episcopate, and the ministry of primacy (here he breaks decisively with Afanasiev in that he does not identify primacy as such with juridical power) is relational.[95] Zizioulas argues that the bishop stands at the head of the community inspired and freely constituted by the Spirit of God, leading it in worship in the Eucharist such that (echoing Ignatius) the bishop is in the people and the people are in the bishop.[96] He expresses himself in the multitude of the faithful, in one place offering the Eucharist to God in the name of the Church, bringing up the "whole Body of Christ" to the "throne of God."[97] The "many" faithful condition the "one" bishop, just as the one bishop does not exist without his particular community.[98] Catholicity, like Khomiakov and Afanasiev, is understood not as a universality enforced on different communities from above and therefore embracing all the particulars in an organized unity but as the wholeness, fullness, and totality of the particulars in themselves as expressed in the "body of Christ 'exactly as' (hosper) it is portrayed in the eucharistic community."[99] This means that each Eucharistic community is catholic because the "whole Christ" is present and incarnate within it, with the one Catholic Church interpenetrating with the catholic churches in various local places.[100] All pyramidal notions of ecclesiology, Zizioulas opines, found within the Western institutional and excessively Christocentric perspective where Christ institutes the Church disappear in the Greek patristic ecclesiology being outlined, since the one bishop and the many in his church (the lay people and the whole presbyterium) form one being co-constituting the Body through the Spirit, and the bishop in no way possesses the fullness of grace and power without these other ministries.[101] This leads Zizioulas to the somewhat surprising claim that, unlike in the West, due to this pneumatological focus on the Church as divine organism and the Eucharist as a corporate event of communion offered up by the community through their bishop, the Eastern Orthodox have no serious problems with clericalism, anti-institutionalism and Pentecostalism.[102]

The Church's relationship to the world, its "mission," is also said to be relational in that the world, from society to the natural creation, is lifted up in gratitude and is in this way sanctified, entering into the life of the Church's communion.[103] Indeed, it is unclear—and here we are reminded of other writers like Tillard and Khomiakov—for Zizioulas where the limits of the Church "can be objectively and finally drawn." The world and the Church interpenetrate in this theology. The world, on the one hand, is God's good creation and never ceases to belong to Him and to rest and to dwell in Him. The Church, on the other hand, is the community, which through the descent of the Spirit transcends in itself the world and offers that world back to God in the Eucharist.[104]

Protestant writers have also contributed to communion ecclesiology.[105] Thus, recently the Oxford Baptist systematic theologian Paul S. Fiddes (b. 1947) has argued that the Church is constituted by the presence of Christ and that this is understood as the "gathered congregation" that Baptists believed is reflected in Matthew 18:20: "where two or three are gathered together in my name, there am I in the midst of them."[106] Furthermore, in the Reformation tradition the Church is the People of God, the new covenant community brought into being through the blood of the new covenant in the cross of Christ. The Baptists added to this idea the notion that the gathered congregation—in which Christ is "presenced" and which is constituted in this way—covenanted themselves with each other so that their union with God is a union with each other. Indeed, Christ gathers them together as His Body, and they respond to His appointment by becoming one with God in Him and with each other so that "they are not just *drawing* together, but *being drawn* together."[107] This movement of loving covenanting communion with God and with one another is the Church, and its foundation is found in God as Trinity. Building creatively on Barth's thought, Fiddes wants to see the relationships of the Trinity as a sort of covenant. The covenant of God with Jesus Christ as the representative human son is identified with the eternal generation of Him by the Father so that God (following Barth) decided to be God a "second time" by binding Himself to be a particular sort of God for us in Christ in a "double covenant of love." Now the covenant of the members of the Church with Christ and with one other "is bound up with that 'covenant' in God's own communion of life in which God freely determines to be God" so that we participate in God's Being, which is an "inner covenant making": "Church is what happens when these vectors intersect, and God in humility opens God's own self to the richness of the intercourse."[108]

Where this interweaving of covenants takes form is in the gathered community's worship. The Church can be understood as a "Eucharistic community" if the Eucharist or Lord's Supper is said to be a central means (though not the only means: e.g., baptism) by which He becomes more deeply present—we might say, united—to the fellowship of believers insofar as Christ uses it "to presence himself."[109] The sharing in the Lord's Supper, then, deepens not just the relationship of Christ with the believer but also the presence of Christ in his "gathered people" so that there is in the gathering a communion or fellowship with Christ and with one another and this is tied to the presence of Christ in the elements.[110] In bread, wine, and, indeed, water (for baptism) the story of Jesus is recalled and He is brought into the present. To be sure, He embodies Himself sacramentally in the Church as He has so promised, and we can regularly be expected to meet Him there; so the Church thereby becomes a gateway into the dance of God's self-covenanting life. This does not mean that God cannot embody Himself in the world, although this need not negate the Church's unique Body. The sacramental understanding of the Church as communion needs to go beyond the believers' bodies into the whole body of the world. From the focus on the Lord's Table we can see God's presence at all tables and in creation, which He continually sustains. We also can see His presence in the broken bodies of prisoners, the thirsty, and the hungry since all bodies can embody Christ and in this way become gateways to the dance of God's life allowing everyone to enter into communion with God and His Church:[111] "All bodies in the world have the potential to be sacramental, awakening us to the presence of the creative and redemptive God, becoming doorways into the flowing relationships that we call Father, Son and Holy Spirit, entrances into the dance of their *perichoresis* of love."[112]

Part II: Ecclesiology *Ad extra*

We now can turn to Latin American liberation theology as well as, more briefly, the various forms of liberation or contextual ecclesiologies that it has produced as examples of ecclesiology *ad extra* or ecclesiologies where the Church is turned in response toward a world that no longer is simply an extension of its boundaries as was the case with Christianity in the past, where Church and Christian civilization or empire overlapped.[113] The ground for liberation theology was prepared for it through two intellectual streams: the ecclesiology of Schleiermacher; and Vatican II's critical affirmation of aspects of modernity as well as its restatement of Catholic social teaching and its (to use the famous phrase) "preferential option for the poor" by which is meant privileging outreach to the hungry, the thirsty, the stranger, widows, orphans, prisoners (Matt. 25:40) and any who suffer injustice because of inequities or systematic evil in society where those in power lord it over those who are disempowered, ignoring their inherent dignity as children of God made in His image.

Friedrich Schleiermacher's monumental systematization of Christian theology, *On the Christian Faith* (1821[114]) is a religion or theology founded, as Brian Gerrish puts it, "within the limits of piety alone," echoing Kant's famous work *Religion within the Bounds of Reason Alone* (1793).[115] If Kant denied access to God through pure (as opposed to practical) reason, then that access, Schleiermacher argued, could be obtained through religion/piety (*Frömmigkeit*) as a modification of feeling. Schleiermacher felt there was a universal feeling of absolute dependence on God as the source of all life and being that was an immediate self-consciousness of God understood as the foundation of all knowing and doing—that is, the "consciousness of being absolutely dependent."[116] God, therefore, is given to us directly in primordial human experience, this feeling of absolute dependence, as almost a sort of intuitive form of divine revelation, the co-existing of God in self-consciousness.[117] Yet the consciousness or feeling never appeared in a general form but was always specific to a particular community. All religions and the communities that embody them, he argued, are accompanied by a unique modification of the feeling of absolute dependence in immediate self-consciousness as a particular form of God-consciousness running the gamut from idolatry as the "lowest" form of religious development to Christianity as the "highest," most fully developed form of self-consciousness having "exclusive superiority" over all other religions.[118] In short, piety, he asserts, is "an essential element of human nature."[119]

The Christian form of the feeling/self-consciousness of absolute dependence is (showing Schleiermacher's Pietist roots) focused on redemption in Christ. Christian theology can only find its bearings as a discipline insofar as it translates into words the feelings particular to Christianity, which have exclusively to do with the redemptive self-proclamation of Christ.[120] In fact, all dogmatic statements incorporated into Christian doctrines "are accounts of the Christian religious affections set forth in speech."[121] Christianity is primarily a soteriological faith: "only through Jesus, and thus only in Christianity, has redemption become the central point of religion."[122] One cannot, therefore, be conscious of God as a Christian without being conscious of redemption in Christ and vice versa.[123] Yet Christ as the Redeemer—and his "redeeming influence" is the primary element of Christian consciousness/religion[124]—redeems us not on the cross but through a communion/fellowship of believers in Christ. Thus it is by the Church alone, as those who share Christian self-consciousness, that one encounters the Redeemer's "unclouded blessedness" and so is saved in this place of "attained perfection, or of the good."[125] What defines Jesus is his "God-consciousness" in that he was perfectly absolutely dependent on God and so required no need for redemption.[126] This power manifested in Christ can be granted to us (who have need for redemption) through our faith in him (which satisfies our need for redemption) by which we obtain the right "impression," which begins saving "faith in God"[127]

But, it may be asked, are there not different Christian communities? Schleier-macher argued that each of these communities—Catholic and Protestant[128]—had a slightly different modification of the Christian version focused on redemption of the universal feeling/self-conscious of absolute dependence on God.[129] The Christian sense of God was always specific to the community of one time and place in which, as Fiddes puts it, "the Redeemer was present to shape and purify this experience."[130] There is no one unchanging essence of the Church (or of theology for that matter), but there are only particular expressions of the general concepts that are in constant flux as the community and its members experience changes. As long as the different communities, Protestant and Roman Catholic, have differences in their respective modifications of the feeling/self-consciousness of absolute dependence on God, there will be different theologies that reflect that unique experience.[131] It should be clear from this account that Schleiermacher's ecclesiology, with its emphasis on the particular experiential character of churches and their theology, is tailor-made for a vision of the Church that wants to express the particular experience of one group, whether that be his own Reform Lutheran Prussian Union Church (created by King Frederick William III of Prussia in 1817 as his state church) or the base or basic church communities of the oppressed and poor of Brazil of the late 1970s, whose experience the controversial Brazilian liberation theologian Leonardo Boff (b. 1938) (to whom we shall return shortly) witnesses, or, to take a contemporary example, the Metropolitan Community Church, which is an American-founded Protestant denomination of 222 churches in 40 countries with a specific ministry to LGBT families and communities.[132]

Yet Schleiermacher's ecclesiology is not the only foundation of the various liberation ecclesiologies that have grown up in the last forty-five years. Vatican II and subsequent papal documents were clearly the inspiration for many developments, particularly of Latin American liberation theology, in emphasizing the work for justice and equality as (what would eventually be described as) "constitutive" aspects of the Christian Gospel. Thus, the 1965 Pastoral Constitution of the Church, *Gaudium et Spes*, famously opens with its affirmation of the Church's solidarity with modern man, especially the poor, in all aspects of his life: "The joys and the hopes, the griefs and the anxieties of the men of this age, especially those who are poor or in any way afflicted, these are the joys and hopes, the griefs and anxieties of the followers of Christ." Nothing human, *Gaudium et Spes* continues, is alien to the Church and does not bring about compassion in it as the Church is a "community composed of men" who are united in Christ led by the Spirit to the Kingdom of the Father toward a salvation that is for all men and so it is bound up intimately with humanity and its history. The Council says that having considered the "mystery of the Church," it now turns toward not only Christians but also the "whole of humanity" so that it can explain to all how it views the presence and activity of the Church in the world today.[133] The Church, like Christ, it said, is called to witness to the truth in the world, to rescue and not sit in judgment, to serve and not be served. But such a task requires the Church to scrutinize "the signs of the times . . . interpreting them in the light of the Gospel."[134] The Church speaks for the People of God, Christ's Body, in affirming its "solidarity, as well its respect and love for the entire human family" and expresses this in its engagement with it in dialogue on the world's various problems.[135] Indeed, "dialogue" might be taken as one of the main themes of the document, from dialogue with atheism to dialogue concerning socioeconomic disputes.[136] Here follows the Council's longest document with pastoral reflections and direction on subjects existential (e.g., death, atheism), social and ethical (e.g., human rights, common good), and practical and political (e.g., unions, private property, war, and peace).

In particular, the document affirms that authentic human freedom is an "exceptional sign of the divine image within man."[137] It therefore affirms the common good of society, understood as the sum of those conditions of social life that allow social groups and their individuals sure access to their own fulfillment, which includes respecting man's universal and inviolable human rights and duties that are necessary for him to lead a truly human life, including food, clothing, shelter, the right to choose a state of life freely and to found a family, education, employment, religious, and so on.[138] The Church is said to proclaim the rights of man by virtue of the gospel and supports contemporary movements that work toward their defense.[139] Far from discouraging the improvement of the social order, the Church urges its constant "improvement" and says that it should be "founded on truth, built on justice and animated by love; in freedom it should grow every day toward a more humane balance."[140] There is a palpable sense in *Gaudium et Spes* that although working toward a more just and equitable society is not strictly identical to the eschatological "consummation of the earth," the "growth of Christ's Kingdom," neither is it irrelevant, and it is of "vital concern" to the Kingdom of God to the extent that it encourages the better ordering of human society. (This passage will in the years following Vatican II be cited repeatedly by liberation theologians.) The Kingdom of God is "eternal and universal, a kingdom of truth and life, of holiness and grace, of justice, love and peace," and it is present on earth in a mystery, but when Christ returns it will come to full flower.[141] Meanwhile, the Church acts as a sort of leaven and soul for human society as it is renewed and transformed into God's family, which impels it to support the causes of justice such as the right to freely found unions and generally a more just economic and labor situation for all men, which means that individuals and governments are morally obliged to feed the hungry, relieve poverty, and share their goods with one another.[142] In this way their life is animated by the "spirit of the beatitudes, notably with a spirit of poverty . . . perfecting the work of justice under the inspiration of charity."[143] As *Lumen Gentium* tells us, the Church is called to carry out her mission like Christ, "in poverty and persecution."[144]

This strong emphasis on justice for all and what would later be called the "preferential option for the poor" was backed up by official teaching throughout the pontificate of Paul VI in the late 1960s through the 1970s. Thus, in Paul VI's encyclical *Populorum Progressio* (1967) (a text very popular with liberation theologians), there is an explicit program to encourage the "People of God" that their mission includes furthering the progress of poorer nations, international social justice, and helping less developed nations help themselves.[145] This is the classic Catholic "social gospel" in its full flower with, among other things, a critique of colonialism, a plea for an equitable distribution of goods, especially private property, an attack on a cold-blooded form of capitalism or "liberalism," an advocating of aid to developing nations, and encouragement of equity in trade relations. Wealthier nations are said to have a threefold moral obligation flowing from the "human and supernatural brotherhood of man" that includes "mutual solidarity" in aiding the poorer nations, "social justice" in rectifying inequitable trading relations, and "universal charity" in building up a more "humane world community."[146] This emphasis on the gospel imperative to work for justice and to, as it were, make the Church's presence ever more realized in the world was further backed up by the 1971 international Roman Catholic Synod of Bishops (the second of its meetings after being established by Paul VI during Vatican II[147]) that, probably for the first time in Roman Catholic magisterial teaching, describes social justice as a "constitutive" aspect of the Christian Gospel: "Action on behalf of justice and participation in the transformation of the world fully appear to us as a constitutive dimension of the preaching of the Gospel, or, in other words, of the Church's mission for the redemption of the human race and its liberation from every oppressive situation."[148]

It is out of this post–Vatican II "social gospel" context as well as a long tradition of native ecclesial co-struggling with the poor (e.g., Bartolomé de las Casas [1484–1586]) that Latin American liberation theology arose. In particular, two episcopal assemblies of the Latin American Roman Catholic Episcopal Conference (*Consejo Episcopal Latinoamericano* [CELAM[149]]) that met to receive and enact Vatican II's teaching were key to its development: Medellín, Columbia (1968), and Puebla, Mexico (1969).[150] At Medellín, the bishops, citing *Gaudium et Spes* and *Populorum Progressio* in particular, pledged to unite themselves with their people ("fraternal solidarity"[151]) who they regularly identify as the "People of God," to contribute to their advancement and to look for a plan of God for Latin America in the (echoing *Gaudium et Spes*) "signs of the times" and "permeate all the process of change with the values of the Gospel."[152] Following a common emphasis in liberation theology on praxis, we are told that it is not enough to theologically reflect on the gospel; evangelical "action is required" as the present was the "time for action," bringing creativity and imagination to bear with the Spirit for new solutions to problems because Latin America was on the threshold of a "new epoch" full of zeal for "full emancipation, of liberation from every servitude, of personal maturity and of collective integration."[153] Particularly crucial in this new age was a message of liberation, solidarity, and justice. This is simply repeating the Gospel of Christ who was sent by His Father to liberate all men from the slavery to which sin has subjected them, including hunger, misery oppression, and ignorance, which are the injustice and hatred born of selfishness.[154] The justice the Church called for was primarily economic and political liberation. It even made a particular plea to businessmen and politicians that social and economic change in Latin America be humanized.[155]

In a famous section, "Poverty of the Church," the bishops called for the Church to embrace spiritual and material poverty in solidarity with the poor and oppressed, following Christ Himself, who, being rich, became poor so through His poverty we might be enriched (2 Cor. 8:9). Christ's mission, it is said, centered "on advising the poor of their liberation and He founded His Church as the sign of that poverty among men." We are told the "poor Church" denounces the unjust lack of this world's goods and the sin that begets it; preaches and lives in spiritual poverty as an attitude of solidarity with the poor and "spiritual childhood and openness to the Lord"; and is bound to material poverty—a poverty that is a "constant factor in the history of salvation." The poverty of the Church is a sign of the "inestimable value of the poor in the eyes of God" and the obligation of solidarity with all those who suffer like them. Their struggles, the bishops say, are the Church's struggles.[156] More than a decade later, despite considerable conservative backlash against this ecclesiology of the "poor Church," the bishops met again at Puebla (1979) and reiterated this same theology, speaking famously of "a preferential option for the poor" as the keystone of the Church's message in Latin America.[157] This basic idea of Catholic social teaching popularized by liberation theology—"the preferential option for the poor"—appears to be one of the central themes of the new pontificate Pope Francis (b. 1936; elected pope March 13, 2013) and seems to reflect the fact that Francis is Latin American as well as a Jesuit (the Jesuits often being proponents of liberation theology).[158]

One of the intellectual architects of Medellín was the Peruvian Dominican theologian Gustavo Gutiérrez (b. 1928), who served as a *peritus* to the Latin American bishops. He is the author of the study that gave the theological movement of liberation theology its name: *A Theology of Liberation* (1971). For Gutiérrez, the Church, as the People of God, not only evangelizes the world but also allows itself to be inhabited and evangelized by that world in which Christ and the Spirit dwell. The Church is not, then, a "nonworld" but simply that part of humanity attentive to the Word who is everywhere present, as we saw earlier with Rahner. As the People of God, the Church dwells in creation and is orientated to the Kingdom promised by Christ and actively works toward it in its liberating praxis.[159]

The emphasis on liberating praxis is a hallmark of Gutiérrez's theological methodology, which is famously influenced (via various European theologians like Jürgen Moltmann [b. 1926] and Johannes B. Metz [b. 1928][160]) by Marxist thinking. He argues that liberation theology reflects with a view to liberating action, "which transforms the present," but it does not do this from an armchair but instead throws itself into the midst of action where God is liberating the poor and the oppressed and throws one's lot in with Him and so sinks its roots "where the pulse of history is beating at this moment" and then subsequently illumines history with the very Word of God, who has likewise committed Himself to the present moment to carry it forward to its fulfillment in the Kingdom. (One is reminded of Marx's witticism: "The philosophers have only *interpreted* the world, in various ways; the point however is to *change* it."[161]) The theology of liberation, therefore, reflects critically on historical praxis in the midst of the battle as if it were of the liberating transformation of the history of mankind and of the Church as that part of humanity that confesses Christ.[162] Truth, then, gives itself not in contemplation but through liberating activity and solidarity with the strugglers. One must reflect on the experience and meaning of the faith from the foundation of one's commitment to abolish injustice and build a new society (a sort of beginning of the eschatological Kingdom), and one's reflection, theology, is verified as true by one's practice of commitment and "by active, effective participation in the struggle which the exploited social classes have undertaken against their oppressors."[163] Thus the Church—and Gutiérrez privileges its identity as the "People of God"—is those people who come to the awareness of the need to commit themselves to a "break with the status quo" or "social revolution," which seems to be identified with a class struggle against capitalism.[164] The long hand of Schleiermacher is evident here because the Church becomes identified with a particular self-consciousness of being engaged with God in liberating the poor, which is reflected in its activity and its distinct theology. It is not surprising, then, that Gutiérrez's theology attracted the attention of an increasingly more conservative Vatican under Pope John Paul II with the Congregation of the Doctrine of the Faith led by Cardinal Joseph Ratzinger (later Pope Benedict XVI). The CDF produced a document in 1984 querying many aspects of liberation theology, especially its "Marxist analysis" of history and theology, and subsequently investigated and even put under censure some of the theologians, including the Brazilian theologian and ex-Franciscan priest Leonardo Boff, the Indian Jesuit theologian Sebastian Kappen (1924–93), and the Sri Lankan theologian and priest Tissa Balasuriya (1924–2013).[165]

With Leonardo Boff's liberation ecclesiology we see a full return to the Schleiermacherian emphasis on the experience of the community as determining its practices and theology, although in this case praxis creates a new ecclesial self-consciousness and accompanying expressive theology.[166] Boff, like Gutiérrez, sees the Church as the People of God.[167] However, he takes this idea one step further by seizing on and developing an idea mentioned by the Medellín

Bishop's Conference, which is that there exists a base community or basic Church whose essential element is its leaders (who can be priests, deacons, religious, or laypeople), which forms the ecclesiastical nucleus of the Church proper.[168] He identified this reality with the "church-of-the-people" or "Church from the Poor" who were involved with the struggle for liberation from the oppressors, both capitalists and military, a struggle that had its analogue in the Christian faith's seeking of ultimate liberation and freedom of the children of God.[169] This struggle of base communities creates a new way of being the Church and of living the Christian faith with the organizing of the Body around the Word, the sacraments (when possible), and around new ministries led by laypeople, though not necessarily negating clerical orders. The power in the community and its exercises of the sacraments is redistributed without centralization and domination, creating a "true democracy of the people" so that everything belongs to the people: "A true 'ecclesiogenesis' is in progress throughout the world, a Church being born from the faith of the poor."[170] This Church *of* and *with* the poor (instead of officialdom's Church *for* the poor[171]) has given a new opportunity for a "new experience of the life of faith," allowing the Church to become completely rethought from the ground up in light of the priority of the Church as a community and sign of liberation.[172] The Church is "reinvented" or "born at the grassroots, beginning to be born at the heart of God's people" so that the experiments by the community gradually confirm their growing self-consciousness and theory of their praxis giving them confidence as a new institution of the "viability of a new way of being church in the world today."[173] Unsurprisingly, although Boff does not reject the traditional offices of bishop, priest, and deacon, he is also in favor of lay celebration of the Eucharist and of women's ordination.[174] Equally unsurprising, he was, due to these controversial opinions and his vision of a dynamic church whose evolving self-consciousness resulted in an evolving set of practices and an evolving ecclesiology, silenced for one year by the CDF in 1985 and not allowed to teach, write, or make public appearances. Under pressure, he eventually left the Franciscan Order and the priesthood in 1992 to write free from magisterial censure and has since married and started a family.

The witness of liberation theology did not go unnoticed in the wider world, and out of its unique emphasis on the revelatory experience of God of the community and the call for gospel action toward effecting justice in society comes a whole series of liberation or contextual theologies reflecting the civil rights movement in the United States of the 1960s onward, the first wave of the feminist movement in the 1970s, the disintegration of colonialism in Asia and Africa after World War II, and the struggle for equal rights by LGBT persons. African American theologians in the United States who were even then participating in the civil rights movement tried to find a theological articulation that might express how the Christian Gospel spoke to the reality of what the American Methodist theologian James H. Cone (b. 1938) referred to, in his classic *A Black Theology of Liberation* (1970), as "black suffering" at the hands of institutionalized regime in a "white racist society," of "white racism" and "white oppression."[175] Like their Latin American counterparts, African American theologians saw Christian theology—for them "black theology"—as a theology of liberation that studied the Being of God in the world "in light of the existential situation of the oppressed community, relating the forces of liberation to the essence of the gospel, which is Jesus Christ."[176] The language used for the black struggle or "Black Revolution" was one of "revolution in America" as it was felt that "the killing and the caging of black leaders has already begun."[177] It must be remembered that while Cone was writing his book, Martin Luther King Jr. (1929–68) had been assassinated in 1968; there was the rise of the black power movement from 1966 onward (e.g., Malcolm X [1925–65]), and the Black Panther Party (1966–82); and there had been race riots in Harlem, New York (1964), and Watts, Los Angeles (1965), and uprisings all over the United States in 1968 following King's assassination.

If God in Christ is conceived in Latin American liberation theology as "poor" and fully identifying with the poor Church, then in black theology God is said to be black. God is a God who is so identified with the oppressed that He makes their experience completely His own. Any other God is said to be a God of racism who is not participating in the liberation of the oppressed from the land.[178] Since the black community is an oppressed community because of its blackness, the Christological importance of Jesus is said to be in His blackness. If Christ is not black like the community He liberates, then the resurrection has no significance for that community: "if he cannot be what we are, we cannot be who he is. Our being with him is dependent on his being with us in the oppressed black condition, revealing to us what is necessary for liberation."[179] Of course, Christ was not literally black but was persecuted and oppressed like the African Americans, so his literal color is not the point. Cone says Christ was not white in any sense of the word but might even be called (following another writer) a "black Jew" or "Black Messiah."[180] The Church, for this sort of theology, is defined wholly by the extent to which it participates in the historical liberation of God of His oppressed people.[181] Salvation is understood in concrete earthly terms as liberation from the injustice inflicted on those who are helpless and poor, which for the black church communities is expressed in the ghetto, so that preaching the gospel is proclaiming to blacks that they do not have to suffer "ghetto-existence."[182] The Church is the place where wounds are being healed and chains are being struck off.[183]

This emphasis on the liberation of minority communities from oppression was applied internationally, and we see the growth during the last forty years of unique ecclesiologies, especially in the African and Asian contexts, that reject the oppression of Western (mostly white European) colonialism.[184] These latter ecclesiologies often attempt to integrate elements of traditional religion and culture into their perspectives, from reverence for ancestors to respect for creation; they are ecclesiologies of the post-Western mission context and are often dealing with a Christianity that negated their experience, language, and culture; they reflect the fact that Christianity is but one of the religions in their locality and sometimes of recent provenance (though this is not necessarily the case: e.g., Ethiopia and India both have Christian communities dating back over a millennium); and they often will reflect the rise of Pentecostalism in world Christianity.

It is in this context that we begin to see theologians thinking together interreligious dialogue and ecclesiology.[185] In the last decade we have seen the emergence of what might be called ecclesiologies of interreligious reflection. These have mostly emerged within the ecumenical movement, especially the World Council of Churches (WCC). In particular, one should note the short WCC discussion paper, "Religious Plurality and Christian Self-Understanding" (2005), which was prepared for the May 2005 Athens meeting of the Conference on World, Mission, and Evangelism and was the result of the work of three groups in the WCC: Faith and Order, Interreligious Relations; and Mission and Evangelism. This paper takes God's "hospitality" to all of creation as its premise and concludes that Christians faced with religious plurality cannot claim salvation uniquely to themselves as if they determined who were saved, for it belongs solely to God, and His providence determines who is saved. Christians only witness to God's offer of hospitality as the "host" of salvation as at an eschatological banquet where mysteriously and humbly He also includes Himself as the "stranger" who is a "guest."[186] At the Ninth Assembly of the WCC in Porto Alegre, Brazil, in February 2006, interreligious dialogue and Christian self-identity was a plenary theme for discussion, and Rowan Williams, then Archbishop of Canterbury, gave the address on this subject.[187]

These discussions continue. The WCC, led by Clare Amos (Programme Executive in Interreligious Dialogue and Cooperation for the WCC), drafted a discussion paper for its Tenth Assembly in Busan, South Korea, in November 2013, on the theme of "Christian self-understanding in the context of religious plurality." With the title, "Who Do We Say that We Are?—Christian Identity in a Multireligious World," this paper is the product of nearly a decade of discussions of various working parties of Christian theologians (including two consultations in 2013 in Switzerland and Kenya) and individual dialogues with particular religious traditions. It is far more explicitly an ecclesiology in light of interreligious encounter than past efforts of the WCC. As its starting point and framework, it takes the doctrine of the Trinity as well as the idea of Christians being graciously reevangelized by their religious neighbors. The document returns repeatedly in different ways to the tension between the uniqueness (sometimes "specificity" or "particularity") and universality of God in Jesus Christ, which the Christian Church proclaims in its gospel and the necessity of encountering the religious Other in order that one's identity can both be tested and enlarged. Indeed, this tension is presupposed by the idea of reevangelization by the religious Other where it is assumed that the truth of God is expressed with fullness in Christ, but at the same time one is impelled to turn to other religions so that we might encounter the gospel anew, hearing in the religious other a new voice of the Word or attaining through such an encounter a fresh insight into our own faith via another "faith."[188] The paper was approved by the Central Committee of the WCC in July 2014 and in a slightly revised form is being sent together with an accompanying study guide to member churches and ecumenical partners for further study, reflection, and discussions.

It was only a matter of time before the situation of identifying Christianity and a community with liberation became a reality for women in America and Europe, who in the late 1960s to early 1970s began fighting for equal civil rights with men. Thus we see in the work of the American Roman Catholic feminist theologian Rosemary Radford Reuther (b. 1936) the same common theme of liberation and struggle against oppression defining the Church's self-consciousness and teaching, but this time the evil faced is not poverty and political oppression or institutionalized racism but the "sin" of patriarchy. The Church in this light becomes a liberation community defined by its liberation from "sexism," which is understood as the ideologies, roles of patriarchy, and social structures enslaved to the same systematic sin. In joining a "feminist liberation Church," one enters a community that puts the struggle against patriarchy and the liberation of woman at the heart of its commitment, self-consciousness, practices, and teaching.[189]

More controversially, liberation theology has been embraced by LGBT Christians. In the wake of the famous Stonewall Riots in New York City in June 1969, there arose the gay rights or gay liberation movement with LGBT persons working for equal civil rights in the United States. Through the influence of this movement in the 1970s and the AIDS crisis of the 1980s, we have seen a Christian response to the pervasive "homophobia" of Western societies with the growth of queer (i.e., gay) theology and, in a few instances, tentative visions of the Church coming from LGBT perspectives. These ecclesiologies embrace gay Christian identity and mark out the Church as a body that is under a direct call by God to be "queer" in a world that enforces a culturally constructed sexual identity of heterosexuality as the "norm" ("heteronormativity"). The Church is seen as the place where these identities are parodied and subverted and a new inclusive Christian identity is given in baptism.[190]

Conclusion

We have arrived at the end of our overview of modern Christian ecclesiology. It has been viewed as simultaneously an internal (*ad intra*) and external discussion (*ad extra*) of who or what the Christian Church is and on how it might, in the spirit of Vatican II, face a world that no longer is simply an extension of its own cultural and religious patrimony, a culture that is post-Christendom and also post-Christian. If Christian theology is to flourish in the new millennium, then it certainly cannot ignore the fact of pluralism, an interreligious world or the increasing ecclesiological attention to the Christian experience of minority groups and non-Western cultures. However, taken to an extreme, these visions of particular groups and how they interpret the community of the Crucified and Resurrected One, Jesus Christ, can easily degenerate into a "wilderness of mirrors" where the unity of the Body as found in the face of its one Head, Christ—"one Lord, one faith, one baptism, one God and father of us all" (Eph. 4:5–6)—can never be seen among the endless proliferation of icons of Christ produced to express the unique experience of different Christian communities.[191] More troubling still, the existence of so many ecclesiologies points to their origin in myriad different visions of Jesus, which further points to multiple versions of the one God so that one must ask oneself whether Christians really do worship the same God.

On the other extreme, communion ecclesiology can degenerate into a self-referential life, a mystic communion of light and grace for the initiated that is consummated in the Eucharist. Such a theology has no reference to the irreducible particularity of the world and other faiths, other than as territory to be annexed for mission until the Church and God is all in all. More scandalously, if "the Eucharist makes the Church" (Henri de Lubac[192]) then how can the Body of Christ claim to be united with its one Head when it manifestly is divided into multiple sniping (even warring) factions? Once again, do these multiple bodies truly worship the same God if they cannot even break bread together? Where indeed is the Body of Christ—the Church—located? Here the two churches with the most universal self-understandings—Roman Catholicism and Eastern Orthodoxy—also have the most developed ecclesiologies of communion where each asserts its identity as the One, Holy, Catholic and Apostolic Church and creates elaborate canonical fences around the sacraments to prevent intercommunion with one another, thus bolstering their privileged self-identity, sacralized self-isolation, and, quite frankly, complete irrelevance to the present age. Most of the Protestant churches and the Anglican Communion, in contrast, practice an open communion where all are invited to the Lord's Table, which, at its extremes, makes communion a celebration not of unity but difference itself. It is as if the Church, in some versions of this sort of ecclesiology, suffering as it does from a lust for relevance, is a Christoform version of contemporary multicultural civil society, an ecclesiological "mosaic" representing everything and therefore signifying nothing in particular, but always faithfully citing Galatians 3:28 as a mantra.[193]

In between these two ecclesiological extremes, contemporary theology needs to steer. On the one hand, it must be aware that it can only be itself, and be one and come to know Jesus Christ as its Body and Head when He leads them in remembering His saving words in the breaking of the bread and the drinking of the cup. Yet these words will and should be received differently in each context and according to the diverse calls and gifts of each community. The limits of interpretation of Christ's words will inevitably be the limits of communion, but these limits need to be negotiated with charity and the assumption that the other party is not willfully distorting the icon of Christ. In contrast, this self-awareness of union in Christ must take in the reality beyond the Church's doors and come into intimate participation with the world the Church believes Jesus has come to unite with in all its difference and particularity. But a union and communion of the Church and the world with no limits becomes meaningless, an abstract universal, so it is just as crucial to realize there are bounds to the Christian Church as it is to be charitable about acknowledging the legitimacy of the interpretation of the Word of God of other Christians and so accepting them in unity. There is no easy and final harmonization of these ecclesiological tensions short of the eschaton, as Christian unity and the Christian Church are not only a divine gift but a created desire for the inconceivable, and where there is desire, there will be difference.

Notes

1. Vatican II was the twenty-first Ecumenical Council by Roman Catholic reckoning. Most of the major Roman Catholic theologians of the twentieth century were official or unofficial *periti* (theological experts) during Vatican II and were responsible for drafting the council documents and written communications and assisting the bishops or council fathers, including Gregory Baum, Louis Bouyer, Marie-Dominique Chenu, Yves Congar, Jean Daniélou, Aloys Grillmeier, Bernhard Häring, Josef A. Jungmann, Hans Küng, Henri de Lubac, Gérard Philips, Karl Rahner, Joseph Ratzinger (later Pope Benedict XVI), and Edward Schillebeeckx. For a history of the council, see Giuseppe Alberigo and Joseph Komonchak, eds., *History of Vatican II*, trans. Matthew J. O'Connell (Maryknoll, NY: Orbis, 1995–2006). See also Herbert Vorgrimler, ed., *Commentary on the Documents of Vatican II* (New York: Herder & Herder; London: Burns & Oates, 1966–67). For an overview, see Joseph Komonchak, "The Significance of Vatican II for Ecclesiology," in *The Gift of the Church: A Textbook on Ecclesiology in Honor of Patrick Granfield, O.S.B.*, ed. Peter C. Phan, 68–92 (Collegeville, MN: Michael Glazer, 2000); and Richard Lennan, "Roman Catholic Ecclesiology," in *The Routledge Companion to the Christian Church*, eds. Gerard Mannion and Lewis S. Mudge, 234–50 (New York: Routledge, 2008).

2. As witness to this, see Yves Congar, *My Journal of the Council*, trans. Mary John Ronayne and Mary Cecily Boulding, ed. Denis Minns (Dublin: Dominican Publications, 2012), 329ff., 352–53, 382–83, 422–24, 559–60, 585–86, 610–12, 629, 675, 727–29, and 771. On Vatican II and other religions, see ibid., 754–57 and commentary at Gavin D'Costa, *Vatican II: Catholic Doctrines on Jews and Muslims* (Oxford: Oxford University Press, 2014).

3. The official ecumenical observers to Vatican II included Jesse Bader, Gerrit Berkouwer, Vitaly Borovoy, Robert McAfee Brown, Fred Corson, Oscar Cullmann, Paul Evdokimov, Georges Florovsky, Frederick Grant, Douglas Horton, Ramban Zakka B. Iwas, George Lindbeck, John Moorman, Nikos Nissiotis, Albert Outler, Bernard Pawley, Edmund Schlink, Alexander Schmemann, Kristin Skydsgaard, Richard Ullmann, Paul Verghese, and Lukas Vischer. Karl Barth was invited to the last session as an observer but could not attend due to ill health; later in September 1966 he made a visit after having studied the council documents in preparation for a seminar at Basel (in the winter semester of 1966–1967) on the Vatican II Constitution on Revelation (*Dei Verbum)* and produced a study (*Ad Limina Apostolorum: An Appraisal of Vatican II*, trans. Keith R. Crim [Edinburgh: St Andrews Press, 1969]).

4. Pope John XXIII, "Pope John Convokes the Council: *Humanae salutis*," December 25, 1961; and "Pope John's Opening Speech to the Council," October 11, 1962," in *The Documents of Vatican II: All Sixteen Official Texts Promulgated by the Ecumenical Council 1963–1965, Translated from the Latin*, ed. Walter M. Abbott (Piscataway, NJ: New Century, 1966), 703–9, 710–19. See also Pope John XXIII, "Pope's [Radio] Address to the Whole World before Council Opens," September 11, 1962, accessed September 25, 2013, http://conciliaria.com/2012/09/popes-address-to-world-month-before-council-opens/.

5. Yves Congar, *True and False Reform in the Church*, trans. and ed. Paul Philibert (1968; repr., Collegeville, MN: Liturgical Press, 2011), 58.

6. Yves Congar, *Power and Poverty in the Church*, trans. Jennifer Nicholson (Baltimore: Helicon, 1964), 136.

7. Karl Rahner, "The New Image of the Church," [1966] in *Theological Investigations*, Vol. 10, *Writings of 1965–67*, Part 2, trans. David Bourke (London: Darton, Longman & Todd, 1973), 3–4.

8. See "Declaration on the Relationship of the Church to Non-Christian Religions" (*Nostra Aetate*) 3, in *The Documents of Vatican II: All Sixteen Official Texts Promulgated by the Ecumenical Council 1963–1965, Translated from the Latin*, ed. Walter M. Abbott (Piscataway, NJ: New Century, 1966), 663; and Yves Congar, *My Journal of the Council* (December 4, 1962), 233. See also, *Acta Synodalia Sacrosancti Concilii Oecumenici Vaticanii II*, Vol. 1, *Periodus Prima, Part IV: Congregationes Generales XXXI–XXXVI* (Vatican: Typis Polyglottis Vaticanis, 1971), 222–27. For the history leading up to this speech, see Léon-Josef Suenens, "A Plan for the Whole Council," in *Vatican II Revisited by Those Who Were There*, ed. Alberic Stacpoole (Minneapolis: Winston Press, 1986), 88–105, accessed September 25, 2013, http://jakomonchak.files.wordpress.com/2012/09/suenens-plan1.pdf.

9. For an overview (and the interconnection of *ressourcement* and *aggiornamento*), see Marcellino D'Ambrosio, "Ressourcement Theology, Aggiornamento, and the Hermeneutics of Tradition," *Communio* 18, no. 4 (Winter 1991): 530–55; see also Gabriel Flynn and Paul D. Murray, eds., with Patricia Kelly, *Ressourcement: A Movement for Renewal in Twentieth-Century Catholic Theology* (Oxford: Oxford University Press, 2012).

10. See A. R. Vidler, *A Variety of Catholic Modernists* (Cambridge: Cambridge University Press, 1970); Bernard Reardon, ed., *Roman Catholic Modernism* (Stanford, CA: Stanford University Press, 1970); Robert D. Haight, "Then *Unfolding of Modernism in France: Blondel, Laberthonnière, Le Roy*," *Theological Studies* 35, no. 4 (1974): 632–66; Gabriel Daly, *Transcendence and Immanence: Study in Catholic Modernism and Integralism* (Oxford: Clarendon Press, 1980); and Darrell Jodock, ed., *Catholicism Contending with Modernity: Roman Catholic Modernism and Anti-Modernism in Historical Context* (Cambridge: Cambridge University Press, 2000). In England, Catholic Modernists included Edmund Bishop (1846–1917), Friedrich von Hügel (1852–1940), and George Tyrrell (1861–1909). In France, among modernist figures are generally said to be Archbishop Eudoxe-Irénée Mignot (1842–1918), Alfred Loisy (1857–1940), Lucien Laberthonnière (1860–1932), Maurice Blondel (1861–1949), and Edouard Le Roy (1870–1954). Lastly, in Italy one counts such writers as Antonio Fogazzaro (1842–1911) and Romolo Murri (1870–1944).

11. See Ralph Del Colle, "Neo-Scholasticism," in *The Blackwell Companion to Nineteenth-Century Theology*, ed. David Fergusson, 375–94 (Oxford: Wiley-Blackwell, 2011); Fergus Kerr, *Twentieth-Century Catholic Theologians: From Neoscholasticism to Nuptial Mysticism* (Oxford: Blackwell Publishing, 2007), 1–16; Fergus Kerr, "A Different World: Neoscholasticism and Its Discontents," *International Journal of Systematic Theology* 8, no. 2 (April

2006): 128–48; Detlef Peitz, *Die Anfänge der Neuscholastik in Italien und Deutschland* (Bonn: Nova et Vetera, 2006); Thomas F. O'Meara, *Church and Culture. German Catholic Theology, 1860–1914* (London: Notre Dame Press, 1992); Gerald A. McCool, *Nineteenth Century Scholasticism: The Search for a Unitary Method*, 2nd ed. (New York: Fordham University Press, 1989); Thomas J. A. Hartley, *Thomistic Revival and the Modernist Era* (Toronto: Institute of Christian Thought, University of St Michael's College, 1971); and Maurice de Wulf, *An Introduction to Scholastic Philosophy: Medieval and Modern: Scholasticism Old and New* (1907; repr., Eugene, OR: Wipf and Stock, 2003).

12. See Kerr, "A Different World," 138. See also Richard A. Peddicord, *Sacred Monster of Thomism: Life and Legacy of Reginald Garrigou-Lagrange* (South Bend, IN: St Augustine's Press, 2004); and Aidan Nichols, *Reason with Piety: Garrigou-Lagrange in the Service of Catholic Thought* (Naples, FL: Sapientia Press, 2008).

13. Kerr, "A Different World," 141–42.

14. Pope Leo XIII, "Aeterni Patris," in *Enchiridion Symbolorum Definitionum et Declarationum De Rebus Fidei et Morum*, 36th edition, ed. Henricus Denzinger and Adolfus Schönmetzer (Barcelona: Herder, 1976), 610–12 (§§3135–40). For English translation, see "Aeterni Patris: Encyclical of Pope Leo XIII: On the Restoration of Christian Philosophy," accessed September 25, 2013, www.vatican.va/holy_father/leo_xiii/encyclicals/documents/hf_l-xiii _enc_04081879_aeterni-patris_en.html.

15. Pope Pius IX, "Quanta cura," in *Enchiridion Symbolorum Definitionum et Declarationum De Rebus Fidei et Morum*, 36th edition, ed. Henricus Denzinger and Adolfus Schönmetzer (Barcelona: Herder, 1976), 574–76 (§§2890–2896); for English translation, see "Quanta cura (Condemning Current Errors)—Pope Pius IX—Encyclical Promulgated on 8 December 1864," accessed September 25, 2013, www.ewtn.com/library/ENCYC/P9QUANTA .HTM.

16. Pope Pius IX, "Syllabus of Errors," in *Enchiridion Symbolorum Definitionum et Declarationum De Rebus Fidei et Morum*, 36th edition, ed. Henricus Denzinger and Adolfus Schönmetzer (Barcelona: Herder, 1976), 576–84 (§§2901–80); for English translation, "The Syllabus: Pope Pius IX," September 25, 2013, www.ewtn.com/library/PAPALDOC/P9SYLL .HTM.

17. "Pastor aeternus," in *Enchiridion Symbolorum Definitionum et Declarationum De Rebus Fidei et Morum*, 36th edition, ed. Henricus Denzinger and Adolfus Schönmetzer (Barcelona: Herder, 1976), 599–601 (§§3065–75). English: "Vatican Council I: *Pastor aeternus*," accessed September 25, 2013, www.ewtn.com/faith/teachings/papae1.htm.

18. See Pope Pius X, *Pascendi Dominici Gregis*: Encyclical of Pope Pius X on the Doctrines of the Modernists, September 8, 1907, accessed September 25, 2013, www.vatican.va /holy_father/pius_x/encyclicals/documents/hf_p-x_enc_19070908_pascendi-dominici-greg is_en.html; see also Pope Pius X, *Lamentabili Sane Exitu*: Syllabus Condemning the Errors of the Modernists, July 3, 1907, www.papalencyclicals.net/Pius10/p10lamen.htm.

19. Pope Pius X, "*Sacrorum Antistitum*," September 1, 1910 (*Motu Proprio* requiring and containing anti-modernist oath), www.papalencyclicals.net/Pius10/p10moath.htm; see also Kerr, "A Different World," 134–36.

20. For personal accounts of this sort of clerical education prior to Vatican II, see Stephen Casey, *The Greater Glory: Thirty-Seven Years with the Jesuits* (Montreal: McGill-Queen's University Press, 2007), 116–72; see also Hans Küng (who underwent the full seven-year formation in Neo-Scholasticism in Rome after World War II), *My Struggle for Freedom: Memoirs*, trans. John Bowden (London: Continuum, 2003), 42–114.

21. See "The Twenty-Four Fundamental Theses of Official Catholic Philosophy," accessed September 25, 2013, www.u.arizona.edu/~aversa/scholastic/24Thomisticpart2.htm; see also Kerr, "A Different World," 131ff.

22. Hans Urs Von Balthasar, "In Retrospect" (1965) in *My Work in Retrospect*, trans. Kenneth Batinovich and Brian McNeil (San Francisco: Ignatius Press, 1993), 89.

23. For a broad overview of modern Catholic theology, see Kerr, *Twentieth-Century Catholic Theologians*.

24. See William V. Dych, *Karl Rahner* (London: Geoffrey Chapman, 1992), 11–12; and Kerr, *Twentieth-Century Catholic Theologians*, 89.

25. On neo-patristic synthesis, see Matthew Baker, "Neopatristic Synthesis and Ecumenism: Towards the 'Reintegration' of Christian Tradition," in *Eastern Orthodox Encounters of Identity and Otherness: Values, Self-Reflection, Dialogue*, ed. Andrii Krawchuk and Thomas Bremer, 235–60 (New York: Palgrave-MacMillan, 2013); Brandon Gallaher, "Georges Florovsky," in *Key Theological Thinkers: From Modern to Postmodern*, ed. Staale Johannes Khristiansen and Svein Rise, 353–70 (Farnham, UK: Ashgate, 2013), Paul L. Gavrilyuk, *Georges Florovsky and the Russian Religious Renaissance* (Oxford: Oxford University Press, 2013); Paul Ladouceur, "Treasures New and Old: Landmarks of Orthodox Neopatristic Theology," *St Vladimir's Theological Quarterly* 56, no. 2 (2012): 191–227; and Aristotle Papanikolaou, *Being with God: Trinity, Apophaticism, and Divine-Human Communion* (Notre Dame, IN: University of Notre Dame Press, 2006).

26. Major figures of Protestant Neo-Orthodoxy included Dietrich Bonhoeffer (1906–45), Emil Brunner (1889–1966), Reinhold Niebuhr (1892–1971), H. Richard Niebuhr (1894–1962), and even Paul Tillich (1886–1965). See Douglas John Hall, *Remembered Voices: Reclaiming the Legacy of "Neo-Orthodoxy"* (Louisville, KY: Westminster John Knox Press, 1998).

27. For discussion, see Christopher Butler, "The Aggiornamento of Vatican II," in *Vatican II: An Interfaith Appraisal*, ed. John H. Miller, 3–13 (Notre Dame, IN: University of Notre Dame Press, 1966); John W. O'Malley, "Reform, Historical Consciousness, and Vatican II's Aggiornamento," *Theological Studies* 32, no. 4 (December 1971): 573–60; and Giuseppe Alberigo, "Réforme ou 'aggiornamento' de l'Eglise?" in *Communion et réunion: Mélanges Jean-Marie Roger Tillard*, ed. G. R. Evans and M. Gourgues (Leuven: Leuven University Press, 1995), 323–32.

28. For example, "Pope Speaks of Unity and the Council," *Criterion* (Indianapolis, Indiana) 1, no. 40 (July 7, 1961): 1, accessed September 25, 2013, www.archindy.org/criterion/files/1961/pdfs/19610707.pdf.

29. Pope Benedict XVI, "Meeting with Bishops Who Participated in the Second Vatican Ecumenical Council and Presidents of Episcopal Conferences—Address of His Holiness Pope Benedict XVI, Clementine Hall, Friday," October 12, 2012, accessed September 25, 2013, www.vatican.va/holy_father/benedict_xvi/speeches/2012/october/documents/hf_ben-xvi_spe_20121012_vescovi-concilio_en.html.

30. See its "Declaration on Religious Freedom" (*Dignitatis humanae*), "Decree on Ecumenism" (*Unitatis redintegatio*), "Declaration on the Relationship of the Church to Non-Christian Religions" (*Nostra aetate*) in *The Documents of Vatican II: All Sixteen Official Texts Promulgated by the Ecumenical Council 1963–1965, Translated from the Latin*, ed. Walter M. Abbott, 675–96, 341–66, and 660–68 (Piscataway, NJ: New Century, 1966); and see commentary at Gavin D'Costa, *Vatican II: Catholic Doctrines on Jews and Muslims* (Oxford: Oxford University Press, 2014); and "Constitution on the Sacred Liturgy," in *The Documents*

of Vatican II: All Sixteen Official Texts Promulgated by the Ecumenical Council 1963–1965, Translated from the Latin, ed. W. Abbott, 137–78 (Piscataway, NJ: New Century, 1966).

31. See Assaad E. Kattan and Fadi A. Georgi, eds., *Thinking Modernity: Towards a Reconfiguration of the Relationship between Orthodox Theology and Modern Culture,* Balamand Theological Conferences 1 (Tripoli, Lebanon: St John of Damascus Institute of Theology; Münster: University of Blamand/Center for Religious Studies, Westfälische Wilhelms-Universität Münster, 2010); Kristina Stoeckl, "European Integration and Russian Orthodoxy: Two Multiple Modernities Perspectives," *European Journal of Social Theory* 14, no. 2 (May 2011): 217–33; Pantelis Kalaitzidis, *Orthodoxy and Political Theology* (Geneva: World Council of Churches, 2012); and Aristotle Papanikolaou, *The Mystical as Political: Democracy and Non-Radical Orthodoxy* (Notre Dame, IN: Notre Dame University Press, 2012).

32. "Message of the Primates of the Orthodox Churches (Phanar, March 6–9, 2014)," 6, accessed September 23, 2014, http://www.patriarchate.org/documents/synaxis-2014-message.

33. For the history of the preparation for the Orthodox "Great and Holy Council," see the work of John Erickson: "Overview of History and Difficulties in Preparing for the Council," in *Orthodox Christianity at the Crossroad: A Great Council of the Church—When and Why,* ed. George E. Matsoukas (New York: Universe, 2009), 19–39; "Episcopal Assemblies and the OCA: A Way Forward?," Orthodox Church in America—Diocese of the West Conference Presentation, October 20, 2010 (manuscript); "Autocephaly and Autonomy," Conference Presentation at "The Forthcoming Council of the Orthodox Church: Understanding the Challenges," Institut Saint-Serge, Paris, October 18–20, 2012 (manuscript, published French translation: "Autocéphalie et autonomie," *Contacts: Revue française de l'orthodoxie,* No. 243 [Juillet–Septembre 2013], 391–412). I am indebted to Professor Erickson for his guidance on this issue and for sharing his work with me.

34. "Message of the Primates of the Orthodox Churches (Phanar, March 6–9, 2014)," 6.

35. See Cyril Hovorun, "The Fragile Promise of the Pan-Orthodox Council," *Catholic World Report,* March 14, 2014, accessed September 23, 2014, http://www.catholicworldreport.com/Item/3001/The_Fragile_Promise_of_the_PanOrthodox_Council.aspx.

36. Johann Adam Möhler, *Unity in the Church or The Principle of Catholicism Presented in the Spirit of the Church Fathers of the First Three Centuries,* trans. Peter C. Erb (Washington, DC: Catholic University of America Press, 1996), 82–84; original: *Die Einheit in der Kirche; oder das Prinzip des Katholicismus, dargestellt im geiste der kirchenväter der drei ersten jahrhunderte,* ed. Rupert Geiselmann (1825; repr., Köln/Olten: Hegner, 1957).

37. Möhler, *Unity in the Church,* 209–12; see also 166ff.

38. See chapter 5 (§36), in Johann Adam Möhler, *Symbolism: or, Exposition of the Doctrinal Differences between Catholics and Protestants as Evidenced by Their Symbolical Writings,* Vol. 2, 2nd ed., trans. James Burton Robinson (London: Charles Dolan, 1847), 258–59; original: *Symbolik, oder Darstellung der dogmatischen gegensätze der Katholiken und protestanten nach ihren öffentlichen bekenntnisschriften,* sixth edition (Mainz/Wien: Florian Kupferberg, 1843), 332–33 (rev.).

39. Möhler, *Unity in the Church,* 212.

40. Ibid., 224, 323; see also 311ff.

41. Ibid., 69; see also, 82.

42. Ibid., 255.

43. Ibid., 209–62.

44. Ibid., 218.

45. Ibid., 255–56.

46. See Michael H. Himes, *Ongoing Incarnation: Johann Adam Möhler and the Beginnings of Modern Ecclesiology* (New York: Crossroad Herder, 1997); Donald J. Dietrich and Michael J. Himes, ed., *The Legacy of the Tübingen School: The Relevance of Nineteenth-Century Theology for the Twenty-First Century* (New York: Crossroad, 1997); Dennis M. Doyle, "Möhler, Schleiermacher, and the Roots of Communion Ecclesiology," *Theological Studies*, 57, no. 3 (1996): 467–80; Dennis M. Doyle, *Communion Ecclesiology: Vision and Versions* (NY: Orbis, 2000); and Hans Boersma, *Nouvelle Théologie and Sacramental Ontology: A Return to Mystery* (Oxford: Oxford University Press, 2009), 41–52.

47. Roger Haight, *Christian Community in History*, Vol. 2, *Comparative Ecclesiology* (London: Continuum, 2005), 292. Haight's volume is the standard recent study of modern ecclesiology. For an overview, see Nicholas M. Healey, "The Church in Modern Theology," in *The Routledge Companion to the Christian Church*, ed. Gerard Mannion and Lewis S. Mudge, 106–26 (New York: Routledge, 2008).

48. "Baptism, Eucharist and Ministry (Faith and Order Paper no. 111, the 'Lima Text')," World Council of Churches, accessed September 25, 2013, www.oikoumene.org/en/re sources/documents/wcc-commissions/faith-and-order-commission/i-unity-the-church-and -its-mission/baptism-eucharist-and-ministry-faith-and-order-paper-no-111-the-lima-text; and "The Church: Towards a Common Vision (Faith and Order Paper no. 214)," World Council of Churches, accessed September 25, 2013, www.oikoumene.org/en/resources/docu ments/wcc-commissions/faith-and-order-commission/i-unity-the-church-and-its-mission /the-church-towards-a-common-vision. See also Thomas F. Best and Günther Gassmann, eds., *On the Way to Fuller Koinonia: Official Report of the Fifth World Conference on Faith and Order, Faith and Order Paper no. 166* (Geneva: World Council of Churches, 1994); Nicholas Sagovsky, *Ecumenism, Christian Origins and the Practice of Communion* (Cambridge: Cambridge University Press, 2000); and Lorelei F. Fuchs, *Koinonia and the Quest for an Ecumenical Ecclesiology: From Foundations through Dialogue to Symbolic Competence for Communionality* (Grand Rapids, MI: Eerdmans, 2008).

49. George Tyrrell, *Christianity at the Cross-Roads*, 2nd impress. (London: Longmans, Green, 1910), 274–75.

50. Yves Congar, "The Mystical Body of Christ" (1937) in *The Mystery of the Church*, trans. A. V. Littledale (London: Geoffrey Chapman, 1960), 118ff.; see also Dennis M. Doyle, "Journet, Congar, and the Roots of Communion Ecclesiology," *Theological Studies* 58, no. 3 (September 1997): 461–79; and Boersma, *Nouvelle Théologie and Sacramental Ontology*, 265–86. The standard study is Gabriel Flynn, *Yves Congar's Vision of the Church in a World of Unbelief* (Burlington, VT: Ashgate, 2004).

51. Yves Congar, "The Church and Pentecost" (1956) in *The Mystery of the Church*, trans. A. V. Littledale (London: Geoffrey Chapman, 1960), 36–37; see also the appendix, 54–57, which has two long selections from Möhler's *Symbolism* (1843) and *Unity in the Church* (1825).

52. See Yves Congar, *Lay People in the Church: A Study for a Theology of the Laity*, trans. Donald Attwater (1953; repr., London: Bloomsbury, 1957).

53. Congar, "The Church and Pentecost," 36.

54. Congar, "The Mystical Body of Christ," 124–27.

55. Congar, "The Mystical Body of Christ," 129–32.

56. Henri de Lubac, *Corpus Mysticum: The Eucharist and the Church in the Middle Ages: A Historical Survey*, trans. Gemma Simmonds with Richard Price and Christopher Stephens, eds. Laurence Paul Hemming and Susan Frank Parsons (Notre Dame, IN: University of

Notre Dame Press, 2007), 88; see also 248–51. See also Dennis M. Doyle, "Henri de Lubac and the Roots of Communion Ecclesiology," *Theological Studies* 60, no. 2 (June 1999): 209–27.

57. Pope Pius XII, "Mystici Corporis Christi: Encyclical of Pope Pius XII on the Mystical Body of Christ," June 29, 1943, 1, accessed September 25, 2013, www.vatican.va/holy_father /pius_xii/encyclicals/documents/hf_p-xii_enc_29061943_mystici-corporis-christi_en.html; original Latin, www.vatican.va/holy_father/pius_xii/encyclicals/documents/hf_p-xii_enc _19430629_mystici-corporis-christi_lt.html.

58. Ibid., 13.

59. Ibid., 103, 5.

60. Ibid., 103.

61. "The Church, in the Word of God, Celebrates the Mysteries of the Christ for the Salvation of the World. Second Extraordinary Synod—The Final Report of the 1985 Extra-ordinary Synod," 2.C.1, accessed September 25, 2013, www.ewtn.com/library/CURIA/SYN FINAL.HTM.

62. Congar, *My Journal of the Council* (October 24, 1964), 642.

63. "Pastoral Constitution on the Church in the Modern World—*Gaudium et Spes*, December 7, 1965, accessed September 25, 2013, www.vatican.va/archive/hist_councils/ii _vatican_council/documents/vat-ii_cons_19651207_gaudium-et-spes_en.html; and *The Documents of Vatican II*, 199–308.

64. Congar, *My Journal of the Council* (October 1, 1963), 328.

65. "Dogmatic Constitution on the Church—*Lumen Gentium*, November 21, 1964, accessed September 25, 2013, www.vatican.va/archive/hist_councils/ii_vatican_council/docu ments/vat-ii_const_19641121_lumen-gentium_en.html; original Latin, www.vatican.va/ar chive/hist_councils/ii_vatican_council/documents/vat-ii_const_19641121_lumen-gentium _lt.html; also *The Documents of Vatican II*, 14–96.

66. See Stephen Bullivant, *The Salvation of Atheists and Catholic Dogmatic Theology* (Oxford: Oxford University Press, 2012); and Stephen Bullivant, *Faith and Unbelief* (Nor-wich: Canterbury Press, 2013).

67. On the meaning of the Roman Church *"subsistit in" Una Sancta* or Universal Chris-tian Church, see "Congregation for the Doctrine of Faith—Declaration 'Dominus Iesus': On the Unicity and Salvific Universality of Jesus Christ and the Church," June 16, 2000, accessed September 25, 2013, www.vatican.va/roman_curia/congregations/cfaith/documents/rc_con _cfaith_doc_20000806_dominus-iesus_en.html; and "Congregation for the Doctrine of the Faith: Responses to Some Questions regarding Certain Aspects of the Doctrine on the Church," June 29, 2007, accessed September 25, 2013, www.vatican.va/roman_curia/congre gations/cfaith/documents/rc_con_cfaith_doc_20070629_responsa-quaestiones_en.html. For a more traditional communion ecclesiology with a strong emphasis on papal primacy, see Joseph Ratzinger, *Called to Communion: Understanding the Church Today*, trans. Adrian Walker (1991; repr., San Francisco: Ignatius Press, 1996).

68. See Karl Rahner, "Anonymous Christians," in *Theological Investigations*, Vol. 6, *Concerning Vatican Council II*, trans. Karl-H. Kruger and Boniface Kruger, 390–98 (London: Darton, Longman & Todd, 1969); Rahner, "Church, Churches and Religions," *Theological Investigations*, Vol. 10, *Writings of 1965–67 2*, trans. David Bourke, 30–49 (London: Darton, Longman & Todd, 1973); Rahner, "Anonymous Christianity and the Missionary Task of the Church," *Theological Investigations*, Vol. 12, *Confrontations II*, trans. David Bourke, 161–78 (London: Darton, Longman & Todd, 1974); Rahner, "Observations on the Problem of the

'Anonymous Christian,'" *Theological Investigations*, Vol. 14, *Ecclesiology, Questions in the Church, the Church in the World*, trans. David Bourke, 280–94 (London: Darton, Longman & Todd, 1976); Rahner, "Anonymous and Explicit Faith" and "The One Christ and the Universality of Salvation," in *Theological Investigations*, Vol. 16, *Experience of the Spirit: Source of Theology*, trans. David Morland, 52–59, 199–224, respectively (London: Darton, Longman & Todd, 1979).

69. Karl Rahner, "Membership of the Church according to the Teaching of Pius XII's Encyclical 'Mystici Corporis Christi,'" in *Theological Investigations*, Vol. 2, *Man in the Church*, trans. Karl-H Kruger, 1–88 (Baltimore: Helicon Press; London: Darton, Longman & Todd, 1963), 82–83. See also Richard Lennan, *The Ecclesiology of Karl Rahner* (Oxford: Clarendon, 1995).

70. Rahner, "New Image of the Church," 19.

71. Jean-Marie Tillard, *Church of Churches: The Ecclesiology of Communion*, trans. R. C. De Peaux (1987; repr., Collegville, MN: Liturgical Press, 1992), 12.

72. Rahner, "New Image of the Church," 18.

73. Ibid., 34–35.

74. See Yves Congar, "La pensée de Möhler et l'Ecclésiologie orthodoxe," *Irénikon* 12, no. 4 (July–August 1935): 320–29; Serge Bolshakoff, *The Doctrine of the Unity of the Church in the Works of Khomyakov and Moehler* (London: SPCK, 1946); and Joseph Famerée, "Orthodox Influence on the Roman Catholic Theologian Yves Congar, OP: A Sketch," *St Vladimir's Theological Quarterly* 39, no. 4 (1995): 409–16.

75. Aleksei Khomiakov, "Some Remarks by an Orthodox Christian concerning the Western Communions, on the Occasion of a Letter Published by the Archbishop of Paris," in *On Spiritual Unity: A Slavophile Reader*, trans. and ed. Boris Jakim and Robert Bird (Hudson, NY: Lindisfarne Books, 1998), 74, 84, 86; see also 79, 81, 89, 110, 126 and 171; original, A. S. Khomiakov, *L'Église latine et le Protestantisme au point de vue de L'Église d'Orient: Recueil d'articles sur des questions religieuses, écrits à différentes époques et à diverses occasions par A. S. Khomiakov* (Vevey, Switzerland: Xenia), 111–64.

76. Khomiakov, "The Church Is One," in *On Spiritual Unity: A Slavophile Reader*, trans. and ed. Boris Jakim and Robert Bird (Hudson, NY: Lindisfarne Books, 1998), 39, 44–45, 46–47, 90 (original, "Tserkov odna" in *A. S. Khomiakov: Sochineniia v dvukh tomakh, Tom 2: Raboty po bogosloviiu* [Moscow: Medium, 1994], 5–23); see also "Some Remarks by an Orthodox Christian [etc.]," 92.

77. Khomiakov, "Letter to the Editor of *L'Union Chrétienne* on the Occasion of a Discourse of Father Gagarin, Jesuit," in *On Spiritual Unity: A Slavophile Reader*, trans. and ed. Boris Jakim and Robert Bird (Hudson, NY: Lindisfarne Books, 1998), 139; original, *L'Église latine et le Protestantisme*, 273–80.

78. Khomiakov, "Some More Remarks by an Orthodox Christian Concerning the Western Communions, on the Occasion of Several Latin and Protestant Religious Publications (excerpts)," in *On Spiritual Unity: A Slavophile Reader*, trans. and ed. Boris Jakim and Robert Bird (Hudson, NY: Lindisfarne Books, 1998), 127; original, *L'Église latine et le Protestantisme*, 165–228.

79. Ibid., 134.

80. Ibid., 121–22.

81. Here, see Michael Plekon, "Nicholas Afanasiev," in *Key Theological Thinkers: From Modern to Postmodern*, ed. Staale Johannes Khristiansen and Svein Rise, 371–78 (Farnham,

UK: Ashgate, 2013); and Aidan Nichols, *Theology in the Russian Diaspora: Church, Fathers, Eucharist in Nikolai Afanas'ev, 1893–1966* (Cambridge: Cambridge University Press, 1989).

82. Nicholas Afanasiev, "The Church That Presides in Love," in *The Primacy of Peter*, trans. Katherine Farrer, ed. John Meyendorff et al. (London: Faith Press, 1963), 75; original, "L'église qui préside dans l'Amour" in *La primauté de Pierre dans L'Eglise Orthodoxe*, ed. N. Afanassieff et al., 7–64 (Neuchâtel: Delachaux et Niestlé, 1960). The title is taken from Ignatius, *Ep. Rom.* pref.

83. See Nicholas Afanasiev, *The Church of the Holy Spirit*, trans. Vitaly Permiakov, ed. Michael Plekon (Notre Dame, IN: Notre Dame University Press, 2007); original, *Tserkov' Dukha Svyatogo* (Paris: YMCA, 1971).

84. Afanasiev, *Church of the Holy Spirit*, 75.

85. Nicholas Afanasiev, *The Lord's Supper by Fr. Nicholas Afanasieff*, trans. and intro. by Fr. Michael J. Lewis (unpublished MDiv thesis, St Vladimir's Orthodox Theological Seminary, Crestwood, NY, May 1988), 32; original, *Trapeza Gospodnia*, L'Orthodoxie et l'actualité, Nr. 2/3 (Paris: Orthodox Theological Institute, 1960); and Afanasiev, *Church of the Holy Spirit*, 87–88.

86. Afanasiev, *Lord's Supper*, 81ff, 165ff, and 270ff. See Yves Congar, "The Historical Development of Authority in the Church: Points for Christian Reflection," in *Problems of Authority: The Papers Read at an Anglo-French Symposium Held at the Abbey of Notre Dame du Bec, in April 1961*, trans. Reginald F. Trevett, ed. John M. Todd, 120–21 (London: Darton, Longman & Todd, 1962); see also his *Power and Poverty in the Church*, 36–39.

87. Afanasiev, *Church of the Holy Spirit*, 16, 34, 136.

88. Ibid., 4–5.

89. Ibid., 255–75.

90. On universal ecclesiology, see Afanasiev, "Church That Presides in Love," 58.

91. Ibid., 110.

92. On "communion ecclesiology," see Douglas Knight, ed., *The Theology of John Zizioulas: Personhood and the Church* (Aldershot: Ashgate, 2007); and Veli-Matti Kärkkäinen, *An Introduction to Ecclesiology: Ecumenical, Historical and Global Perspectives* (Downers Grove, IL: IVP Academic, 2002), 95–102.

93. John Zizioulas, "The Church as Communion," in *The One and the Many: Studies on God, Man, the Church, and the World Today*, ed. Gregory Edwards (Alhambra, CA: Sebastian Press), 51, 59.

94. Ibid., 52–53.

95. Ibid., 53–57.

96. John Zizioulas, *Being as Communion: Studies in Personhood in the Church* (1985; repr., Crestwood, NY: St Vladimir's Seminary Press, 1997), 137. See Ignatius, *Ep. Smyrn.* 8.

97. Zizioulas, *Being as Communion*, 153.

98. Ibid., 137.

99. Ibid., 149.

100. Ibid., 157.

101. Ibid., 139–40; regarding the bishop as the pinnacle of catholicity, see 153ff.

102. Ibid., 140.

103. Ibid., 57–58.

104. Ibid., 162.

105. For other examples of Protestant Communion ecclesiology, see Dietrich Bonhoeffer, *Communio sanctorum: A Theological Study of the Sociology of the Church*, trans. Reinhard

Krauss and Nancy Lukens, ed. Clifford J. Green (1930; repr., Minneapolis: Fortress Press, 2009); Emil Brunner, *The Misunderstanding of the Church*, trans. Harold Knight (London: Lutterworth, 1952); Miroslav Volf, *After Our Likeness: The Church as the Image of the Trinity* (Grand Rapids, MI: Eerdmans, 1998); and Veli-Matti Kärkkäinen, "The Church as the Fellowship of Persons: An Emerging Pentecostal Ecclesiology of Koinonia," *Pentecostal Studies* 6, no. 1 (2007): 1–15.

106. Paul S. Fiddes, *Tracks and Traces: Baptist Identity in Church and Theology*, Studies in Baptist History and Thought, Vol. 13 (Carlisle, UK: Paternoster Press, 2003), 158–59.

107. Ibid., 76–78.

108. Ibid., 78–80. See also Karl Barth, *Church Dogmatics*, eds. G. W. Bromiley and T. F. Torrance, Vol. 2, part 2 (Edinburgh: T.&T. Clark, 1957), 161ff.

109. Fiddes, *Tracks and Traces*, 158–59.

110. Ibid., 168.

111. Ibid., 173–74, 190–91.

112. Ibid., 174. For an earlier statement of Fiddes's Trinitarian theology, see his *Participating in God: A Pastoral Doctrine of the Trinity* (Louisville, KY: Westminster John Knox Press, 2000). See also his recent major work, *Seeing the World and Knowing God: Hebrew Wisdom and Christian Doctrine in a Late-Modern Context* (Oxford: Oxford University Press, 2013).

113. For an overview, see Christopher Rowland, ed., *The Cambridge Companion to Liberation Theology* (Cambridge: Cambridge University Press, 1999); Kärkkäinen, *An Introduction to Ecclesiology*, 163–230; and Gerard Mannion and Lewis S. Mudge, eds., *The Routledge Companion to the Christian Church* (Oxford: Routledge, 2008), 273–494.

114. Other editions include 1822, 1884.

115. Brian Gerrish, *A Prince of the Church: Schleiermacher and the Beginnings of Modern Theology* (London: SCM Press, 1984), xiii; and Immanuel Kant, "Religion within the Boundaries of Mere Reason" [1793], in *Religion within the Boundaries of Mere Reason and Other Writings*, ed. and trans. Allen Wood and George Di Giovanni (Cambridge: Cambridge University Press, 1998).

116. Friedrich Schleiermacher, *The Christian Faith*, 2 vol., Vol. 1, trans. and ed. H. R. MacKintosh and J. S. Stewart (New York: Harper & Row, 1963), 12 (§4); original: *Der Christliche Glaube: Nach den Grundsätzen der evangelischen Kirche im Zusammenhange Dargestellt* (Halle: Otto Hendel, 1895).

117. Ibid., 1:17 (§4.4); 1:126 (§30.1).

118. Ibid., 1:33 (§7.2).

119. Ibid., 1:26 (§6.1).

120. Ibid., 1:92 (§19, post.).

121. Ibid., 1:76 (§15).

122. Ibid., 1:56 (§11.3).

123. Ibid., 1:261 (§62.3).

124. Ibid., 1:57 (§11.4).

125. Ibid., 2:431–38 (§101); 2:527 (§113). See also Christoph Dinkel, *Kirche gestalten: Schleiermachers Theorie des Kirchenregiments* (Berlin: Walter de Gruyter, 1996); and Adele Weirich, *Die Kirche in der Glaubenslehre Friedrich Schleiermachers* (Frankfurt am Main: Peter Lang, 1990).

126. Schleiermacher, *The Christian Faith*, 1:385–89 (§94).

127. Ibid., 1:68 (§14.1); see also 1:70 (§14.2).

128. His account of Orthodoxy, in typically nineteenth-century German orientalist fashion, sees it as a sort of Catholic intellectual backwater with more incense and icons. See ibid., 1:101–2 (§23).

129. Ibid., 1:101ff (§23).

130. Fiddes, *Tracks and Traces*, 4.

131. Ibid., 5.

132. Leonardo Boff, *Ecclesiogenesis: The Base Communities Reinvent the Church*, trans. Robert R. Barr (1977; repr., London: Collins, 1987), 34ff. See also the Metropolitan Community Churches website: http://mccchurch.org, accessed September 25, 2013.

133. *Gaudium et Spes*, 1.

134. Ibid., 3–4.

135. Ibid., 3; see also 40.

136. Ibid., 21, 68.

137. Ibid., 17.

138. Ibid., 26.

139. Ibid., 41.

140. Ibid., 26.

141. Ibid., 39.

142. Ibid., 68, 69.

143. Ibid., 72.

144. *Lumen Gentium*, 8.

145. Pope Paul VI, "*Populorum progressio:* Encyclical of Pope Paul VI, On the Development of Peoples," March 26, 1967, 5, accessed September 25, 2013, www.vatican.va /holy_father/paul_vi/encyclicals/documents/hf_p-vi_enc_26031967_populorum_en.html, Compare Pope Paul VI, "*Octogesima Adveniens:* Apostolic Letter of Paul VI," May 14, 1971, accessed September 25, 2013, www.vatican.va/holy_father/paul_vi/apost_letters/documents /hf_p-vi_apl_19710514_octogesima-adveniens_en.html. Also see Pope Paul VI, "*Evangelii nuntiandi:* Apostolic Exhortation of His Holiness Pope Paul VI," December 8, 1975, accessed September 25, 2013, www.vatican.va/holy_father/paul_vi/apost_exhortations/documents /hf_p-vi_exh_19751208_evangelii-nuntiandi_en.html. More recently, see the Pontifical Council for Justice and Peace's *Compendium of the Social Doctrine of the Church*, June 29, 2004, accessed September 25, 2013, www.vatican.va/roman_curia/pontifical_councils/just peace/documents/rc_pc_justpeace_doc_20060526_compendio-dott-soc_en.html; and Pope Benedict XVI, "Encyclical Letter, *Spe Salvi* of the Supreme Pontiff Benedict XVI," accessed September 25, 2013, www.vatican.va/holy_father/benedict_xvi/encyclicals/documents/hf _ben-xvi_enc_20071130_spe-salvi_en.html.

146. Pope Paul VI, *Populorum progressio*, 44.

147. Pope Paul VI, "Apostolic Letter Motu proprio. *Apostolica Sollicitudo* establishing the Synod of Bishops for the Universal Church," September 15, 1965, accessed September 25, 2013, www.vatican.va/holy_father/paul_vi/motu_proprio/documents/hf_p-vi_motu-prop rio_19650915_apostolica-sollicitudo_en.html.

148. "Justice in the World: 1971 Synod of Bishops," accessed September 25, 2013, www .shc.edu/theolibrary/resources/synodjw.htm. See also Kärkkäinen, *An Introduction to Ecclesiology*, 175.

149. "*Consejo Episcopal Latinoamericano:* CELAM," accessed September 25, 2013, www.celam.org.

150. Second General Conference of Latin American Bishops, *The Church in the Present-Day Transformation of Latin America in the Light of the Council. II. Conclusions* (Medellín Conference) 3rd ed. (Washington, DC: Secretariat for Latin America, National Conference of Catholic Bishops, 1979); and Third General Conference of Latin American Bishops, *Puebla: Evangelization at Present and in the Future of Latin America. Conclusions* (London: Catholic Institute for International Relations, 1979). For *CELAM—Conferencias Generales*, see www .celam.org/conferencias_gen.php, accessed September 25, 2013.

151. Second General Conference, *Church in the Present-Day Transformation*, 19–20.

152. On the "People of God," see, for example, 41. See also ibid., 19–20.

153. Ibid., 27.

154. Ibid., 33.

155. Ibid., 37.

156. Ibid., 174–76.

157. Third General Conference, *Puebla*, 178–81.

158. See Pope Francis, "Audience to Representatives of the Communications Media: Address of the Holy Father Pope Francis, Paul VI Audience Hall, Saturday," March 16, 2013, accessed September 25, 2013, www.vatican.va/holy_father/francesco/speeches/2013/march /documents/papa-francesco_20130316_rappresentanti-media_en.html; and "Address of Pope Francis to the Students of the Jesuit Schools of Italy and Albania, Paul VI Audience Hall, Friday, 7 June 2013," accessed September 25, 2013, www.vatican.va/holy_father /francesco/speeches/2013/june/documents/papa-francesco_20130607_scuole-gesuiti_en.html; and Antonio Spadaro, "A Big Heart Open to God: The exclusive interview with Pope Francis," September 30, 2013, accessed September 4, 2014, http://americamagazine.org/pope -interview ("Discernment is always done in the presence of the Lord, looking at the signs, listening to the things that happen, the feeling of the people, especially the poor"). Note in the last two pieces cited the reference by Pope Francis to the same letter of Pedro Arrupe (1907–91), a famous former superior general of the Jesuits (1965–83), concerning the need to experience poverty to relieve it. Arrupe is often credited with coining the expression "the preferential option for the poor."

159. Gustavo Gutiérrez, *A Theology of Liberation: History, Politics and Salvation*, trans. and ed. Caridad Inda and John Eagleson (1971; repr., London: SCM Press, 1985), 260–61.

160. See Jürgen Moltmann, *Theology of Hope: On the Ground and Implications of a Christian Eschatology*, trans. James W. Leitch (London: SCM Press, 1967), based on the 5th German-language ed., 1965; and Johannes B. Metz, *Theology of the World*, trans. William Glen-Doepel (London: Burns & Oates, 1969).

161. Karl Marx, "Theses on Feuerbach" (1845), XI in *The Marxist Reader: The Most Significant and Enduring Works of Marxism*, ed. Emile Burns (New York: Avenel Books, 1982), 192–95.

162. Gutierrez, *A Theology of Liberation*, 15.

163. Ibid., 307.

164. Ibid., 102, 137–38.

165. "Congregation for the Doctrine of the Faith—Instruction on Certain Aspects of the 'Theology of Liberation,'" accessed September 25, 2013, www.vatican.va/roman_curia/con gregations/cfaith/documents/rc_con_cfaith_doc_19840806_theology-liberation_en.html. See also the earlier document of the CDF: "Ten Observations on the Theology of Gustavo Gutiérrez (3/83)," in *Liberation Theology: A Documentary History*, ed. A. J. Hennelly, 348–50 (Maryknoll, NY: Orbis: 1990). See also Sebastian Kappen, *Jesus and Freedom* (Maryknoll, NY:

Orbis, 1977); and Sebastian Kappen, *Liberation Theology and Marxism* (Puntamba: Asha Kendra, 1986); and Tissa Balasuriya, *Mary and Human Liberation: The Story and the Text* (1990; repr., London: Mowbray, 1997).

166. Compare Boff to the work of Juan Luis Segundo: *The Community Called Church*, Vol. 1, trans. John Drury (1968; repr., Maryknoll, NY: Orbis, 1973); and *Theology and the Church: A Response to Cardinal Ratzinger and a Warning to the Whole Church,* trans. John W. Diercksmeier (Minneapolis: Winston Press, 1985).

167. Leonardo Boff, *Church, Charism and Power: Liberation Theology and the Institutional Church*, trans. John W. Diercksmeier (1981; repr., London: SCM Press, 1985), 132ff.

168. Boff, *Ecclesiogenesis*, 15.

169. Ibid., 12; and Boff, *Church, Charism and Power*, 7, 8.

170. Ibid., 9.

171. Ibid., 10.

172. Ibid., 134.

173. Boff, *Ecclesiogenesis*, 23, 33.

174. Ibid., 61ff.; and ibid., 76ff.

175. James H. Cone, *A Black Theology of Liberation* (Philadelphia: J. B. Lippincott, 1970), 22, 24–25. Cf. Delores S. Williams, *Sisters in the Wilderness: The Challenge of Womanist God-Talk* (Maryknoll, NY: Orbis, 1993), 204–34; Diana L. Hayes, *And Still We Rise: An Introduction to Black Liberation Theology* (Mahwah, NJ: Paulist Press, 1996); Robert Beckford, *Dread and Pentecostal: A Political Theology for the Black Church in Britain* (London: SPCK, 2000); and Anthony Reddie, "Black Ecclesiologies," in *Routledge Companion to the Christian Church*, ed. Gerard Mannion and Lewis S. Mudge (Oxford: Routledge Press, 2007), 443–60.

176. Cone, *Black Theology of Liberation*, 17.

177. Ibid., 220, 33, 35.

178. Ibid., 120–21, 116.

179. Ibid., 213.

180. Ibid., 218.

181. Ibid., 230.

182. Ibid., 227, 226, 233, 231.

183. Ibid., 237.

184. On the African context, see John S. Mtibi, *African Religions and Philosophy*, 2nd ed. (1969; repr., Oxford: Heinemann, 1990); J. N. K. Mugambi and Laurenti Magesa, *The Church in African Christianity: Innovative Essays in Ecclesiology* (Nairobi: Initiative Publishers, 1990); Bengt Sundkler and Christopher Steed, *A History of the Church in Africa* (Cambridge: Cambridge University Press, 2000); Cephas N. Omenyo, "Essential Aspects of African Ecclesiology: The Case of the African Independent Churches," *Pneuma* 22, no. 2 (2000): 231–48; Kärkkäinen, *An Introduction to Ecclesiology*, 194–201 (with bibliography on African Independent Churches); and Steve de Gruchy and Sophie Chirongoma, "Earth, Water, Fire and Wind: Elements of African Ecclesiologies," in *Routledge Companion to the Christian Church*, ed. Gerard Mannion and Lewis S. Mudge (Oxford: Routledge, 2007), 291–305. On the Asian context, see Aloysius Pieris, *An Asian Theology of Liberation* (1986; repr., New York: Continuum, 2006); and Aloysius Pieris, *Love Meets Wisdom: A Christian Experience of Buddhism* (Maryknoll, NY: Orbis, 1987). See also Thomas C. Fox, *Pentecost in Asia: A New Way of Being in Church* (Maryknoll, NY: Orbis, 2002); Peter C. Phan, ed., *Christianities in Asia* (Oxford: Wiley-Blackwell, 2011); Peter C. Phan, *Christianity with an Asian Face: Asian American Theology in the Making* (Maryknoll, NY: 2003), 171–83; and Peter C. Phan, "The Church

in Asian Perspective," in *Routledge Companion to the Christian Church*, eds. Gerard Mannion and Lewis S. Mudge (Oxford: Routledge, 2007), 275–90.

185. See Peter C. Phan, *Being Religious Interreligiously: Asian Perspectives on Interfaith Dialogue* (Maryknoll, NY: Orbis, 2004); see also Gerard Mannion, *Ecclesiology and Postmodernity: Questions for the Church in Our Time* (Collegeville, MN: Liturgical Press, 2007), 75–101.

186. "CWME Preparatory Paper No. 13: Religious Plurality and Christian Self-Understanding," World Council of Churches, May 15, 2005, accessed September 25, 2013, www.oikoumene.org/en/resources/documents/other-meetings/mission-and-evangelism/pre paratory-paper-na-13-religious-plurality-and-christian-self-understanding.

187. Rowan Williams, "WCC Assembly Plenary on Christian Identity and Religious Plurality," Ninth Assembly of the WCC, Porto Alegre, Brazil, World Council of Churches, February 17, 2006, accessed September 25, 2013, www.oikoumene.org/en/resources/documents /assembly/2006-porto-alegre/2-plenary-presentations/christian-identity-religious-plurality /rowan-williams-presentation.

188. "Who Do We Say That We Are?—Christian Identity in a Multireligious World," Document No. GEN PRO 02, World Council of Churches Central Committee, July2–8, 2014, Geneva, Switzerland (thanks to Dr. Clare Amos for providing me a copy of this document); I was a part of one of the working groups on this paper led by Clare Amos in Nairobi, Kenya, in February 2013, which included (among others) S. Mark Heim, Dagmar Heller, Veli-Matti Kärkkäinen, Douglas Pratt, Marianne Moyaert, and Jesse Mugambi.

189. Rosemary Radford Reuther, *Sexism and God-Talk: Towards a Feminist Theology* (London: SCM Press, 1983), 201; and Rosemary Radford Reuther, *Woman-Church: Theology and Praxis of Feminist Liturgical Communities* (San Francisco: Harper & Row, 1988). Cf. Elizabeth Schüssler Fiorenza, *In Memory of Her: A Feminist Theological Reconstruction of Christian Origins*, 2nd ed. (London: SCM Press, 1999), 285–342. For a more recent feminist ecclesiology, see Natalie K. Watson, *Introducing Feminist Ecclesiology* (London: Sheffield Academic Press, 2002); and Natalie K. Watson, "Feminist Ecclesiology," in *Routledge Companion to the Christian Church*, ed. Gerard Mannion and Lewis S. Mudge (Oxford: Routledge, 2007), 461–75.

190. See Sally Gearhart and William R. Johnson, eds., *Loving Women/Loving Men: Gay Liberation and the Church* (San Francisco: Glide Publications, 1974); George R. Edwards, *Gay/Lesbian Liberation: A Biblical Perspective* (New York: Pilgrim Press, 1984); J. Michael Clark, *A Place to Start: Toward an Unapologetic Gay Liberation Theology* (Dallas: Monument Press, 1989); Michel Foucault, *History of Sexuality: An Introduction*, Vol. 1, trans. R. Hurley (Harmondsworth, UK: Penguin, 1990); Robert Goss, *Jesus Acted UP: A Gay and Lesbian Manifesto* (San Francisco: HarperSanFrancisco, 1993); Nancy Wilson, *Our Tribe: Queer Folks, God, Jesus, and the Bible* (New York: HarperCollins, 1995); James Alison, *Faith beyond Resentment: Fragments Catholic and Gay* (New York: Crossroad, 2001); and Gerard Loughlin, ed., *Queer Theology: Rethinking the Western Body* (Oxford: Wiley-Blackwell, 2007), 63–96. Also see the site "Queering the Church: Towards a Reality Based Theology," http://queeringthe church.com, accessed September 25, 2013.

191. On "wilderness of mirrors," see T. S. Eliot, "Gerontion," in *The Complete Poems and Plays 1909–1950* (New York: Harcourt, Brace & World, 1971), 23.

192. de Lubac, *Corpus Mysticum*, 88.

193. "There is neither Jew nor Greek, there is neither slave nor free, there is neither male nor female; for you are all one in Christ Jesus" (Gal. 3:28).

Scripture Dialogue VII
Continuity and Change in the Church

Acts 15:1–29

Commentary

Acts ("The Acts of the Apostles") was written by Luke as the sequel to his gospel. Starting from the ascension of Jesus, Acts tells of the growth and spread of the early Church, with particular emphasis, in its second half, on the missionary work of Paul, largely among Gentiles. The following passage, from the middle of Acts, refers to the "Council of Jerusalem," at which a momentous decision is made about the grounds on which Gentiles could become members of the Church. Earlier in Acts (chapter 10), Luke records how God led an initially reluctant Peter to go beyond the boundaries of his own Jewish people and preach Christ to Gentiles. A question that then arose was what should be expected of such Gentile converts. One view was that they should keep the whole Law of Moses (vv. 1 and 5). Paul and Barnabas argued against this position, and the disagreement prompted the meeting described in the following passage, at which, crucially, Peter and James spoke in support of Paul and Barnabas and this view prevailed. A letter expressing the Council's decision was then sent to Gentile believers. It would be hard to overstate the significance of this decision for the overwhelmingly Gentile community that the Church was soon to become. (Consider the path of history if the meeting had decided the other way.) It is also worth considering how difficult, and theologically controversial, the process of reaching this decision must have been, with the "rigorist" group presumably believing that the teaching of scripture was being lightly set aside; James, significantly, appeals to a scriptural passage (from the prophet Amos) in favor of the Pauline position. As we consider how believers seek the will of God while negotiating change in continuity with their tradition, an interesting phrase occurs at verse 28, where the letter states that the decision reached was one that "seemed good to the Holy Spirit and to us." How exactly this was discerned is not stated, but what is clear is the confidence that processes of human deliberation can work in harmony with the guidance of God's Spirit.

Biblical text:

[1]Then certain individuals came down from Judea and were teaching the brothers, "Unless you are circumcised according to the custom of Moses, you cannot be saved." [2]And after Paul and Barnabas had no small dissension and debate with them, Paul and Barnabas and some of the others were appointed to go up to Jerusalem to discuss this question with the apostles and the elders. [3]So they were sent on their way by the church, and as they passed through both Phoenicia and Samaria, they reported the conversion of the Gentiles, and brought great joy to all the believers. [4]When they came to Jerusalem, they were welcomed by the church and the apostles and the elders, and they reported all that God had done with them. [5]But some believers who belonged to the sect of the Pharisees stood up and said, "It is necessary for them to be circumcised and ordered to keep the law of Moses."

[6]The apostles and the elders met together to consider this matter. [7]After there had been much debate, Peter stood up and said to them, "My brothers, you know that in the early days God made a choice among you, that I should be the one through whom the Gentiles would hear the message of the good news and become believers. [8]And God, who knows the human heart, testified to them by giving them the Holy Spirit, just as he did to us; [9]and in cleansing their hearts by faith he has made no distinction between them and us. [10]Now therefore why are you putting God to the test by placing on the neck of the disciples a yoke that neither our ancestors nor we have been able to bear? [11]On the contrary, we believe that we will be saved through the grace of the Lord Jesus, just as they will."

[12]The whole assembly kept silence, and listened to Barnabas and Paul as they told of all the signs and wonders that God had done through them among the Gentiles. [13]After they finished speaking, James replied, "My brothers, listen to me. [14]Simeon has related how God first looked favourably on the Gentiles, to take from among them a people for his name. [15]This agrees with the words of the prophets, as it is written,

[16]'After this I will return,
and I will rebuild the dwelling of David,
which has fallen;
from its ruins I will rebuild it,
and I will set it up,

[17]so that all other peoples may seek the
   Lord—
even all the Gentiles over whom my name
   has been called.
Thus says the Lord, who has been
   making these things [18]known from long ago.'

[19]Therefore I have reached the decision that we should not trouble those Gentiles who are turning to God, [20]but we should write to them to abstain only from things polluted by idols and from fornication and from whatever has been strangled and from blood. [21]For in every city, for generations past, Moses has had those who proclaim him, for he has been read aloud every sabbath in the synagogues."

[22]Then the apostles and the elders, with the consent of the whole church, decided to choose men from among their members and to send them to Antioch with Paul and Barnabas. They sent Judas called Barsabbas, and Silas, leaders among the brothers, [23]with the following letter: "The brothers, both the apostles and the elders, to the believers of Gentile origin in Antioch and Syria and Cilicia, greetings. [24]Since we have heard that certain persons who have gone out from us, though with no instructions from us, have said things to disturb you and have unsettled your minds, [25]we have decided unanimously to choose representatives and send them to you, along with our beloved Barnabas and Paul, [26]who have risked their lives for the sake of our Lord Jesus Christ. [27]We have therefore sent Judas and Silas, who themselves will tell you the same things by word of mouth. [28]For it has seemed good to the Holy Spirit and to us to impose on you no further burden than these essentials: [29]that you abstain from what has been sacrificed to idols and from blood and from what is strangled and from fornication. If you keep yourselves from these, you will do well. Farewell."

Scripture Dialogue VIII
Continuity and Change in the Umma

Qurʾān 2:142–44

Commentary

See the comments on the change of *qibla* in Scripture Dialogue II. It is apparent from this passage that the change of *qibla* provoked significant public comment, some of it critical. The Qurʾānic response addresses these comments and affirms the divine purpose in the change. Here, as elsewhere in the Qurʾān, change in the life of the community is mandated by the authority of direct divine revelation. Other examples in the Qurʾān of changes in the practice of the community mandated by divine revelation include the command to fight (from around the same period as the change of *qibla*—see 2:216–17) and the stages toward a full prohibition of wine.

Qurʾānic text:

¹⁴²The foolish of the people will say: What hath turned them from the *qiblah* which they formerly observed? Say: Unto God belong the East and the West. He guideth whom He will unto a straight path.

¹⁴³Thus We have appointed you a middle nation, that ye may be witnesses against mankind, and that the messenger may be a witness against you. And We appointed the *qiblah* which ye formerly observed only that We might know him who followeth the messenger, from him who turneth on his heels. In truth it was a hard (test) save for those whom God guided. But it was not God's purpose that your faith should be in vain, for God is Full of Pity, Merciful toward mankind.

¹⁴⁴We have seen the turning of thy face to heaven (for guidance, O Muhammad). And now verily We shall make thee turn (in prayer) toward a *qiblah* which is dear to thee. So turn thy face toward the Inviolable Place of Worship, and ye (O Muslims), wheresoever ye may be, turn your faces (when ye pray)

toward it. Lo! Those who have received the Scripture know that (this revelation) is the Truth from their Lord. And God is not unaware of what they do.

Ḥadīth: the use of *ijtihād*

Commentary

This ḥadīth addresses the context of how the community should order its common life (focused here in the work of a judge) in the absence of directly relevant divine revelation. The ḥadīth affirms that where there is no guidance available from the Qur'ān and the Sunna (as recorded in the Ḥadīth), then it is correct to practice *ijtihād*. The status of this ḥadīth is debated, as is the meaning of *ijtihād*, but it is generally understood as the application of human reasoning to the demands of a new situation, drawing on the principles of Islamic legal thought. Here, then, we have a recognition of how the challenges of change in the life of the community will need to be addressed using human reason as well as the sources of divine revelation.

Ḥadīth text:

Muʿādh reported that when God's Messenger sent him to Yemen, he asked him how he would judge [i.e., decide cases].

> He said: "I will judge in accordance with God's Book (the Qur'ān)."
> The Prophet asked him: "What if it is not found in the Book of God?"
> Muʿādh replied: "Then [I would judge] according to the *sunnah* of God's Messenger."
> The Prophet then asked: "And if it is not found in the *sunnah* of God's Messenger?"
> Muʿādh replied: "I will make a judgement based on my own interpretive effort (to apply *ijtihād*)."

> The Prophet said: "Praise belongs to God, Who has made the messenger of the Messenger of God consistent with what pleases him.[1]

Note

1. Narrated by Ahmed 22161, Abu Dawud 3592, Tirmidhi 1332. See http://www.islami city.com/articles/Articles.asp?ref = IC0107-322.

PART IV

Reflection

Conversations in Doha

LUCINDA MOSHER

W hile Building Bridges seminars always include a series of fine lectures, at their core is the lively and frank conversation encouraged by the intentional use of small-group discussion of a collection of preassigned texts. This essay offers a brief description of the small-group process, then shares some of the highlights of Building Bridges 2013's conversations organized around this seminar's three overlapping themes: the nature and purpose of the community of believers; its unity and disunity; and its experience of continuity and change.

Building Bridges participants are assigned to one of four break-out groups. These groups remain constant throughout the seminar, and a moderator encourages everyone to contribute to the conversation. A session begins with a few moments of silence, followed by reading aloud the passage(s) of scripture to be studied. Each member then raises up a phrase (or even a single word) that had caught his or her attention especially, perhaps mentioning a question it raised. Sometimes the urge to offer lengthy explanation or to jump in with a question is overwhelming; but when the method is honored and discussion is deferred until each person has identified a compelling word or phrase, participants appreciate its "gathering and centering" value. Out of the resulting theological reflection, interpenetrating themes emerge.

The Nature and Purpose of the Community of Believers

Four of Building Bridges 2013's eight break-out sessions were devoted to passages of scripture pointing to the nature and purpose of Church and *Umma*. Some participants admitted that it is often a challenge to understand the other community in its own vocabulary. Several suggested that *jamāʿa* might be better than *umma* as a parallel to *ekklesia* when speaking comparatively of a community understood as bound by worship of God in an agreed upon manner. "The Qurʾānic language about *umma* is more functional than Biblical language about community," someone asserted; "the Qur'ānic language focuses on how the community should act." One Muslim called *umma* "a strong word" with many subdivisions, such as *madhāhab* (schools of jurisprudence) and *jamaʿāt* (congregations), and it need not refer to human communities. "There are *ummat* [nations] of animals," he pointed out. Another Muslim noted that *jamāʿa* appears more often than *umma* in traditional sources; furthermore, *umma* terminology is too often misused in the modern period.

Under this theme are topics such as chosenness, identity, covenant, and obedience. A Christian cautioned that "it is not that suddenly in the New Testament we see God being merciful." The Exodus narrative, another Christian noted, includes stories of human unfaithfulness but yet makes clear that "God does not stop being faithful because we are unfaithful." A Muslim nodded, pointing out that "the Qur'ān has many verses indicating God's mercy outweighs God's wrath, overwhelms God's anger."

In shifting their attention to Romans 11, one group noted how belief has been understood as a gift. "There is a deep theological tension between faith as a gift and willful disobedience," one person noted. Another asked whether the key question in this passage is "Why haven't Jews accepted Christianity?" or "What is the status of Jews who haven't accepted Christ?" The Christian respondent suggested that, rather, Paul (a Jew himself) "is struggling to see how God remains faithful to the promises He made to Israel. Paul is also admonishing Christians against arrogance."

In Romans, someone asserted, "Law is very important, and we shouldn't think that Paul abolishes it. Law is a gateway to Christ. But Paul thinks that through Christ you enter a life of obedience, not the other way around." In opposition to this view, one participant said that, in this passage, "obedience and disobedience mean belief and disbelief; it is not a question of law." Yet another Christian insisted that "it is a question of love primarily; not primarily of law. Even disobedience is part of God's plan so that He may be merciful. Disobedience is part of God's plan to make the covenant universal."

Continuing discussion of Romans 11, a Christian noted that Paul presumes all will come together in the end. "One God, one faithfulness, one covenant. Paul wonders why all are not *one* yet! God's got something going on here. Paul is reluctant to side with those who think all Jews should become Christian or those who think all Christians need to become Jews first." In one group, consideration of Romans 11 led to Muslim questions about the history of the early Jewish-Christian community. How strong was its identity? How long did it continue? Another asked about Christian anti-Semitism. When did it emerge? To what extent was it fed by economics or politics?

Another group explored the rhythms of being *called to* God and *sent by* God. "The calling is based on a reciprocal covenant with God in the divine economy that is mutual but asymmetric." The transformation of this ancient covenant, by means of the patrimony of Abraham, was discussed in some detail. Someone noted that Jews, Christians, and Muslims all have used "Abraham" to dispossess the others. Christianity began as a Jewish movement, but Christians then developed an alternative spiritual-covenant community by which they became co-heirs of and with Christ in the Holy Spirit, forming action groups as vanguards, vehicles, and mediums of personal and social transformation. The prophet of Islam was called upon by the Qur'ānic revelation to rekindle the spirit of the Christian covenant and revive the law (both positive and prohibitive) of the Abrahamic covenant.

Pointing to the conditional statements of Exodus 19:5 ("if you obey my voice"; "if you keep my commandment"), one Christian noted how easily this might be translated into a particular legal or ritual form. "Yet the Old Testament prophets keep reminding us that God is not so interested in ritual behavior. Rather, God is interested in our being loving. Consider Matthew's parable of the sheep and the goats [Matt. 25:31–45]. The sheep and goats ask the same questions and get very different answers!" This group dug further into the notion of law as the dual commandment to love God and neighbor versus law as the Ten Commandments. "Christians are not unethical," one said; "they simply mean that the Law can't *save* you. Only God's grace can save you. It's not things you do to get into the saved community. It's the things you do *because* you are in there!" A Muslim nodded, saying that in Islam, there is a similar need to balance Sharī'ah with *taṣawwuf* (spirituality).

Reading Ephesians 4:1–16 raised many questions about love as opposed to judgment, about love as a challenge for believers, about the boundary between insiders and outsiders. Muslims in one group found this passage puzzling—particularly its assertion that Christ "descended into the lower parts of the earth." What does this mean? "According to Christian tradition, between his death and resurrection, Jesus descended to the underworld to redeem all people before him," a Christian explained. "There is cosmic oneness with, and redemption of, people who came even before the Christian community was formed."

The Epistle to the Ephesians speaks of "the body of Christ." One Muslim asked: "Does 'body' mean the physical body of Christ or the body of people following Christ?" It is describing the community's ontological and social one-ness, someone answered, following this with an explanation of the use of "body language" in the Hellenistic world in which this epistle was written. "*Body* is a term that comes from surrounding societies; it is used both metaphorically and sociologically. The emphasis is quite material. The sufferings of the communal body are the sufferings that Christ still undergoes." A Muslim pointed to a similar concept in Islam. "There is a ḥadīth that states, 'Muslims are a body. When one hurts, the whole body hurts.'" A Christian mentioned Aquinas's teaching that "every single person in humanity is part of this body, but some parts of this body have not yet come into operation. That is how Aquinas under-stands those who don't yet believe in Christ, who aren't a part of the body of Christ."

In discussing Q. 2:120–45, considerable attention was given to 2:143, which speaks of God's mercy and boundless power. "We have appointed you a middle nation," this verse begins—thus implying other nations. Is a "middle nation" a mediator? If so, that would be an intriguing notion, someone commented. To one group, a "middle nation" seemed to some to refer to the way the commu-nity interacts with another community as a blessing. "This is about lived reli-gion as a modeling that changes hearts and affects others," one woman observed; "it is the notion that my blessing and generosity affects others." A Christian described Islam as "a priestly people sharing God's grace." This would be "a very Christian way of looking at it," a Muslim countered, "but it makes sense nevertheless." The main point, another suggested, is that "a middle com-munity is not neutral; it is a critique of extremes."

One of the Christians inquired about Q. 2:139: "Say (unto the People of the Scripture): Dispute ye with us concerning God when He is our Lord and your Lord? Ours are our works and yours your works. We look to Him alone." It is "a complicated short verse," one Muslim responded. This is Pickthall's translation; "there are other ways to translate it." For example, someone noted, Abdel Haleem renders this passage: "Say [Prophet] [to the Jews and Christians], 'How can you argue with us about God when He is our Lord and your Lord? Our deeds belong to us, and yours to you. We devote ourselves entirely to Him.'"[1] "It's a better translation," he asserted; "in it, 'We' is expansive and inclusive."

Discussion moved to Q. 3:113–15 and 5:66, both of which are about "People of the Scripture" (as Pickthall puts it). A specific contingent, "people who are moderate," is the subject of 5:66. "This verse voices an expectation that people will be true to their own scripture, that they will follow their own law," one Muslim explained; "Christians are not expected to become Muslims."

When the Qur'ān speaks of "best community" (as it does in 3:110), a Christian wanted to know, what does this term mean? *When* is one the best community? Is it dependant on the community's actions? *Who* is the "best community"? Muslims? Someone suggested that the "best community" could be *mu'minūn* (believers)—a more encompassing term that includes some Christians and Jews with Muslims. Another pointed to a related verse: "If God had so willed, He would have made you one community. . . . So vie with one another in good works" (5:48). "So often," she noted, "diversity can be a trial, something to overcome. But according to this verse, diversity can be good. The only practical thing to do in the face of frustration is to compete in good works." Someone else asked about the next clause: "Unto God ye will all return, and He will then inform you." A Muslim explained that this is a recurring theme in the Qur'ān. "It is meant for Muslims and non-Muslims; it is open-ended. There is no need to argue theology with other groups." Another suggested it means that "what God has planned and what we *perceive* that God has planned may be quite different," noting that Ibn 'Arabī writes about plurality at the level of the world versus plurality at the level of the divine attributes. "This is related to free will," someone said; "God's permission and God's approval are two different things," said another.

Unity and Disunity

"John 17 is fascinating to me!" one Muslim woman exclaimed; "the notion of mystical union with God has resonance with Islamic mystics." A Christian man nodded: "In this passage from John, the 'I' and the 'you' don't get annihilated. Unity is not a loss but an enabling of the self." A Muslim man noted that "I in you" language is strong in Platonic thought, but there it has more to do with the psychological, with self-transformation. In John, however, we are drawn into the mysterious. "The early Sufis talk like this," he noted.

Discussion of John 17 led inevitably to more questions regarding the Christian doctrine of the Trinity. Someone asked whether the Trinitarian language in John led to Christian disunity. Since oneness in community is emphasized in Islam in both the modern and premodern periods, a Muslim admitted that he struggled to understand John 17:22–23; he wondered: in this passage, in what sense is "one" meant? "Does this imply one group? Does the word 'one' in Greek have different nuances? What sort of reasoning is going on here?" A Christian responded that, of the canonical Gospels, John has the simplest Greek but the most complex ideas. By contrast, 1 Corinthians 1:10–17 is an example of Paul's appealing in a straightforward way for resolution of disagreements in the early Christian community. This group noted that 1 Corinthians 1:10–17 highlights the difference between ideal and reality, thus unity versus disunity. As does John 17, one noted, the 1 Corinthians passage "ends with a 'punch in the face' that sends you back to think some more." One Catholic pointed out that John 17:20 ("I ask not only on behalf of these, but also on behalf of those who will believe in me through their word") is used in the canon of the Mass. "It is used ritually in community." One Christian noted that "some commentaries on John 17:20 assert that, in saying 'I ask not only on behalf of these [the disciples], but also on behalf of those who will believe in me through their word,' Jesus is in effect praying in the Garden of Gethsemane for the believing community now, in the twenty-first century."

A Muslim asked about John 17:22 ("So that they may be one, as we are one"), noting that, "Jesus seems to be speaking about two very different kinds of oneness here!" In reply, a Christian recalled that "Thomas Aquinas said that the human church can never be *one* in the way that Christ and the Father are one because that is a unity of essence. It has to be unity of mind, of praise; not ontological identity." Another Christian nodded. "This passage is talking about unity rather than sameness," she explained; "union is not absorption." Her colleague continued, "John's point is that the notion of being in this community is taken very seriously. Outside of this community you are not connected to divine glory."

1 Corinthians, one Christian pointed out, provides insight into the nature of some of the divisions in the early Church: What does it mean to "belong to" a person? What does it mean to baptize "in the name of" someone? "The Greek text says 'I am *of* Paul,'" one Christian explained; "it's genitive. If we take it as past, it could mean 'I got into the club via this guy.' If belonging is mere identity with a faction or a mediator, then it is problematic." Another Christian noted that the Roman Catholic Church uses John 17 to say that as long as there is disunity institutionally, we cannot participate in the sacraments together. Too often we have unity that excludes differences. Among Christians, there's no unity on what is meant by "unity."

Moving on to Q. 4:59, which speaks of obeying "those in authority," Muslims at one table agreed that it is a contentious verse: Shi'ites differ with Sunnis as to where to put the punctuation; authority is understood differently in the Shi'ite and Sunni traditions. "In Shi'ite Islam, the imāms have authority" one explained; "in the contemporary era, the ayatollahs act on behalf of the Hidden Imām." Authority is also understood differently in the mystical and legal strands of Islam, someone else pointed out. "Authority is sometimes divided into three categories: theological, legal, and spiritual. But Salafism asks you to abandon all established schools of law, theology, and spirituality."

"Those in authority" (Q. 4.59) is an easy verse to exploit, another Muslim asserted. Who is "in authority"? Scholars? Political leaders? As defined by whom? "Authority" has no uniform meaning. "Deference to political authority, even corrupt political authority, is perpetuated to this day as a result of this verse," yet another Muslim said.

Taking up Q. 49:9–13, a Christian observed that this passage suggests that divisions are part of God's plan. "However, it also raises the question: What's the power of knowing, in light of God as Knower?" A Muslim explained that 49:9 is more about actual violence (physically killing) rather than legal matters. "We are to fight the party that refuses peace initiatives, 'until they return to the ordinance of God.'" But, someone wondered, "doesn't that imply a theological dimension?" "This really is about quarrelling," the Muslim responded; "the part about the ordinance of God seems to indicate that the feuding parties are to seek help from authorities."

It was noted that Ibn Majah 2:1303 #3950 (among the texts assigned for this session) is the ḥadīth used as authority for "consensus." It recognizes the centrality of God's authority but also recognizes that it has to be mediated. This raises the question: Who can adjudicate? Shi'ite Islam has a clearer structure of authority, but even so, there can be difference of interpretation. The Sunni tradition locates authority in the 'ulamā', but theirs is a derived, diffused authority and is linked to consensus. One Muslim explained that, by the end of the second Islamic century, authority was located in the four schools of law. During the third to the twenty-ninth centuries, two Sunni schools of theology predominated. With regard to spiritual matters, authority came to be located in the ṭarīqas. "Now, he lamented, "we have Salafi, who discard all the schools of law and say, 'Listen only to us!'" Another Muslim concurred: "There has always been a problem of authority in Sunni Islam. Many think that as long as they have studied, they don't need any formally given authority to interpret."

Continuity and Change

Taking up the theme of change involved close reading of the Acts 15 account of the "Council of Jerusalem"—for which the core issue was the grounds on which Gentiles could become full members of the Church. A Muslim pointed to Acts 15:28 ("For it seemed good to the Holy Spirit and to us . . .") and wondered how the term "Holy Spirit" is being used here, and asked, "Why is there mention only of the Holy Spirit here? Why is there no mention of Christ?" What is the function of the Holy Spirit in maintaining community? Someone observed that verses 20 and 28 each mention four prohibitions from the Law of Moses that are to be sustained, but verse 28 lists these prohibitions in a different order from verse 20; he wondered, "Why this difference?" Yet another Muslim, referring to the whole account, asked his group: "Why these details?" Such questions generated much discussion of "change of custom" versus "change of theology."

A method of discernment is at play in this passage from Acts, a Christian explained. The warrant for change comes from events attributed to the Holy Spirit, to observable experience. In issuing his response to what the gathering has heard from Paul, Barnabas, and Simeon, James quotes from the prophet Amos. "Early Christians looked for the face of Jesus in Jewish scriptures," this Christian explained. "See Irenaeus's *Apostolic Preaching*. He makes no reference to Christian writings; all of his references are to Jewish texts." One group noted that the story of the Council of Jerusalem is, at one level, a story of the contrast between faith and action. It raises questions about the nature of Torah; it also raises questions about the nature of the Church: is it inclusive or exclusive?

Readings for the theme of change included a ḥadīth in which the Prophet Muhammad commends *ijtihād* (human reasoning) as a third option (after turning to the Qur'ān and the Sunnah) for judges making decisions about community life. "Qur'ān and Sunnah are mentioned as distinct here," one Muslim noted; "but they really aren't." Notice that the Prophet asks a man *how* he would judge, urged another Muslim: "this is about practical, not theological, matters. It is about how he would apply *ijtihād*." This ḥadīth summarizes what change is allowed or acceptable in Islam; it helps to answer the question, "What are the principles of Islamic legal thought?" Generally, explained one Muslim, "You are to turn your face toward truth as one created by God according to a pattern. The pattern is unalterable. Islam is understood, therefore, as restoration of unalterable human nature. The fundamentals hold true and steady. Only the legal details change. *Fiqh* (jurisprudence), then, is the effort to understand the cosmic plan."

Discussion of continuity and change in the *umma* led some to consider the relationship of Islam to other religions. "The Prophet of Islam led by example," one Muslim explained, "remaining impartial even under pressure when asked to arbitrate on the cases brought to him in Medina." Another Muslim noted that Ibn ʿArabī speaks of stability within constant fluctuation: stability of essence, fluctuation of form. "He says it is the height of arrogance to say that the other religions are abrogated by Islam," she explained. After all, "the Sun does not abrogate the light of the stars." Someone noted that Shafiʿī, the great legal scholar, had argued that Zoroastrians were People of the Book. Another reminded the group of Reza Shah-Kazemi's book making the case that Buddhism has common ground with Islam, and that Sachiko Murata has written on the relationship of Taoism to Islam.[2] Regarding the relationship between Islam and Hinduism, a Muslim explained that it has been argued that Advaita Vedanta has scripture; thus followers of this path are not like the polytheists of Mecca: "General Hajjaj called a council and decided that adherents of Advaita Vedanta were People of the Book. Moghul emperor Jalaluddin Akbar followed this precedent regarding Hindu Sindh.[3] Christians who participated in conquest didn't have to pay poll tax. Akbar eliminated poll tax for Hindus and Sikhs in army and government."

Conclusion

During the closing plenary, two particularly interesting conclusions emerged. The first was that the faith community binds what wouldn't ordinarily be bound; the default position is fragmentation, actually. The second conclusion was that talking about community per se is nigh unto impossible because "community" is not an entity in itself; it is tied to everything else. No wonder, then, that our discussion of community had been wide ranging, with deep exploration of many topics not explicitly on the agenda for Building Bridges 2013—far broader than what is reported here.

Notes

1. M. A. S. Abdel Haleem, translator, *The Qurʾān* (Oxford: Oxford University Press, 2004), 22.

2. Reza Shah-Kazemi, *Common Ground between Islam and Buddhism: Spiritual and Ethical Affinities* (Louisville, KY: Fons Vitae, 2010); and Sachiko Murata, *The Tao of Islam: A Sourcebook of Gender Relationships in Islamic Thought* (Albany: State University of New York Press, 1992).

3. General al-Hajjaj al-Yusuf (d. 714 CE) was an Umayyad strategist instrumental in Muslim expansion into the Sindh and the Punjab. Jalaluddin Akbar lived 1542–1605.

Index

CPSIA information can be obtained at www.ICGtesting.com
Printed in the USA
LVOW10s0249220415

435516LV00003B/45/P